FAITH-BUILDING *stories*

May God bless you

Ruth Palau Silvoso

FAITH-BUILDING
stories

FROM OUR HOME & FROM AROUND THE WORLD

BY RUTH PALAU SILVOSO

FAITH-BUILDING STORIES
by Ruth Palau Silvoso

TRANSFORM OUR WORLD
P.O. Box 20310
San Jose, CA 95160-0310

ISBN: 978-1-7923-3495-5

Cover & Book Design by i6 Graphics, LLC
www.i6graphics.com

Printed in Santa Clara, CA, USA
First Edition

Contact for bulk and wholesale purchase:
ruthsilvoso@transformourworld.org

www.transformourworld.org

CONTENTS

FOREWORD

In *Faith-Building Stories*, Ruth, who is the youngest of my five sisters, shares memorable recollections of our early and happy childhood outside Buenos Aires, Argentina.

Ruth vividly tells how our businessman father and devoted mother lived their lives for His glory and motivated us by example to bring thousands to eternal life through Jesus Christ. What a blessing to have had a father and mother who as a couple, and parents, both loved the Lord.

It's thrilling to read page after page of answers to prayer, many supernatural in nature during intensely dramatic moments of need.

Ruth and her husband, Ed Silvoso, have ministered in many nations, and you've probably heard them in person during one of their trips. You will especially appreciate and delight in reading their stories and reviewing their case studies.

Read and be encouraged, and then pass this book on to friends and colleagues to share the blessing!

Dr. Luis Palau

MARILYN & RUTH

PROLOGUE
A DAUGHTER'S TRIBUTE

When I think of my mom, one of the first things that comes to mind is her gift for telling stories in an engaging way. However, when she most comes to life is when she is telling us faith-building stories. Whether actual Bible stories, stories from the British missionary movement of the 19th century (which her mother faithfully shared with her and her siblings), or the hundreds of stories, both big and small, from our family's spiritual journey through the years, they all inspire faith and strengthen us in our walk with God.

I wish you could have the added blessing of hearing her tell them in her own voice with her captivating inflections and facial expressions, but what is most important is to receive the infusion of faith and hope that flows from recounting the great things that God has done, both in ordinary and extraordinary circumstances and people throughout time.

It was one such story that the Lord used to lead me to Christ when I was five-years-old. We were living in Argentina at the time, and my mom and I had stayed home alone one morning, which was very rare as the ministry kept our family extremely busy. My mom called me into her bedroom to tell me a story. She pulled out her Bible and began to read the story of Zaccheus with great enthusiasm and emotion. I particularly recall when she got to the part where Jesus called to him and said, "'Zaccheus, hurry and come down, for today I must stay at your house.' And he hurried and came down and received Him gladly."

I literally leapt to my feet and told her, "I want Jesus to come to my house today, too!"

She led me in the salvation prayer and I remember feeling just like Zaccheus, overflowing with joy to have the Lord in the home of my heart forever! We didn't know at the time that I would be six feet tall once fully grown, but the Lord has such a sense of irony to use the story of a famously short man to lead this tall woman to invite the Lord into her heart like he did.

I pray your faith increases as you read through this collection of glory stories, and may you be inspired each day to recount to those around you the great things He has done and continues to do!

Marilyn (Silvoso) Schuler

INTRODUCTION

We all have sweet memories of stories we were told in our childhood that, even though they were shared a long time ago, continue to water our souls. We hear a lot of bad news these days that withers our soul. This is why we need to hear more good news and uplifting testimonies to nurture ourselves and, especially, our children.

It is always good to remember what the Lord has done because that is always a source of great encouragement. The stories in this book are not mere recollections; they are living and uplifting testimonies of God's faithfulness that give Him all the glory.

When my six siblings and I were growing up, my mother often shared anecdotes of heroes of the faith that sustained our faith when we were facing major difficulties. I vividly remember the one about George Mueller, the director of the Ashley Down Orphanage in Bristol, England. On one occasion, the orphanage's house-mother informed him, "The children are dressed and ready for classes but there is no food for them to eat breakfast."

Mr. Mueller told her to take the 300 children into the dining room and instruct them to be seated at the tables. He then led them in thanking God for the food they were about to receive. From a human perspective, what he did was ridiculous, but being the man of faith that he was, he was fully convinced that God would provide food for the children as He had done before. Within minutes, a baker knocked on the door.

"Mr. Mueller," he said, "last night I couldn't sleep. I had a feeling that you would need bread this morning. I got up and baked three batches for you. Can I bring them in?"

Soon there was another knock at the door. It was the milkman. His cart had broken down right in front of the orphanage and the milk would spoil by the time it could be fixed. He asked Mr. Mueller if he could use some free milk. Mr. Mueller smiled as the milkman brought in ten large containers. It was just enough for the 300 hungry children!

As you can imagine, hearing those testimonies during our formative years—when we were dealing with the typical insecurities of growing up while living in a country where social uncertainty, political instability and economic chaos were common occurrences—provided a solid anchor to weather those storms and lead us to safe harbors.

By God's grace, what He has done in and through our family, today is touching millions with the good news of the Gospel, and the source of that ocean at high tide is none other than our wonderful mother, Matilde Balfour Palau, who didn't just make time to tell us stories, but turned faith-building storytelling into a lifestyle. Some evenings we sat in the living room to listen to her read from a book, but more often than not, she just shared them "on the go," as she was cooking, ironing, or on the way to visit someone who was sick or needed encouragement.

Those inspiring testimonies turned into the raw material from which our characters and ministries were forged, and all her children grew up to become dedicated servants of God. My older brother, Luis Palau, has preached the Gospel to millions. My sister Matilde is one of the most effective personal evangelists I know. Martha married Juan Carlos Ortiz, a well-known revivalist and author of the book *Disciple*, and they have planted churches and blessed multitudes. Ketty has preached the Gospel all over and continuously blesses people with her gift of helps. Margarita (closest to me in age) married Miguel Angel Pujol—a businessman and social entrepreneur—and with him she is bringing transformation to the city of Corrientes, Argentina, where in addition to ministering to high level influencers, they also have a mercy ministry to the most needy.

> Those inspiring testimonies turned into the raw material from which our characters and ministries were forged.

Along with my husband Ed, we lead a global network of thousands of influencers that take the power and the presence of God to their spheres of influence to see lives and cities transformed. And my younger brother, Jorge, is an accomplished musician who enables parishioners to worship God to the tune of the music he so exquisitely plays on the church organ every weekend, in addition to being a marketplace minister in the judicial system.

More than a storyteller, my mother *was* the story…yes, the fascinating story of a woman who became a widow at a very young age and successfully raised seven children in some of the most difficult and challenging circumstances. Her faith, anchored in God, was not left in the hull of the ship, but instead her inspiring stories connected it to sails that caught the wind of the Spirit that carried her children to safe ports from where they all became ministers.

God has blessed Ed and me with four precious daughters who have married wonderful men and given us twelve amazing grandchildren. All of them are not only walking with God, they are on fire for Him, taking His power and His presence to where they live and work, validating the Bible promise we find in Acts 16:31, "Believe in the Lord Jesus, and you will be saved, you and your household."

It was only natural to carry on the storytelling legacy of my mother, so when our daughters were young, I would always bring a special story from our trips to build their faith and to help explain some of the reasons for us being away from home. Besides being excited about receiving a gift or souvenir from our trips, they were always interested in the stories since it made them feel like they were a part of the ministry.

Today, our grandkids ask us, "Can you tell us about your trip? Do you have a special story to tell us?"

I'm so glad my daughters encouraged me to create this collection of stories so that not only our family, but families around the world can continue to share in this godly legacy.

In this book I present a selection of faith-building stories to inspire you to believe that no matter how fierce the storm, and how strong the winds, you, too, can walk on water toward Jesus. And even if you occasionally sink, as Peter did, Jesus will pick you up and walk with you to the boat. And when that happens, the storm will calm down and those in the boat will be strengthened, as my siblings and I were when my mother held our hands in the midst of life's storms.

Read on, and be blessed to become a blessing to others.

PART 1

STORIES OF OUR FAMILY & EARLY YEARS IN MINISTRY

1 THE FATHER WHO WENT TO HEAVEN

My ancestors migrated from Europe to Argentina. On my mother's side, they came from France and Scotland, and on my father's side, from northern Spain (Cataluña to be exact). So, as my husband Ed likes to say, "We were assembled in Argentina using European parts!"

My mother was from a well-to-do family. She met my father, an already prosperous and good-looking young man, when they both lived in Ingeniero Maschwitz, a quaint little town north of Buenos Aires, the nation's capital. After setting eyes on her, my dad would ride his horse by her house every afternoon at the same time to greet her as a demonstration of his interest. My mother, of course, also took notice of when he would ride by, and would come to the door to return his greeting, albeit more discreetly. When my maternal grandfather learned about this budding romance, he didn't approve because my dad-to-be wasn't of British stock. But this changed when a good Englishman friend of his told him that my dad was a respected businessman.

Finally, my grandpa relented, grew to like my dad, and my parents were married in the Catholic Church. At the time, they didn't know Jesus as their personal savior, but eventually, first my mother, and then my dad, were led to the Lord by a British executive with the Shell Oil Company who spent all his non-working hours doing missionary work.

My dad was expanding his business and my mom's life grew busier and busier with a new child born every two years, but filled with excitement about their newfound faith, they enthusiastically preached the Gospel to everybody they ran into. Many neighbors came to the Lord, and on weekends they took some of those converts to neighboring towns to witness by distributing Gospel tracts and inviting people to a tent they had set up in an empty lot. There my mom would play a portable pump organ while the new believers sang evangelistic songs and my dad would preach. Those that received the Lord were taught the basics of the faith and then baptized in a makeshift baptistry next to the tent. Once a group of new believers was established, my dad would build them a chapel. They planted nine churches, all of which are still in existence today.

Everything looked very promising: they had a thriving business with many employees, a lovely home, a growing family, rental properties and a lot of land on which my dad planned to build more houses. But without warning, my dad contracted pneumonia and died at the very young age of 34. Toward the end, he was delirious with a fever that would not break. On his last day on earth, he sat up in bed and sang a song that went like this: "There are crowns, there are crowns, the palm branch of victory waiting for me." And then he closed his eyes and went to be with the Lord whom he had loved and served so well.

I never met my father because my mom was five months pregnant with me at the time of his death, but growing up I heard time and again about his faith, his service for the Lord, and his passion for evangelism and church planting. Even though I never felt his hands caressing me, or his strong arms holding me up, or his voice soothing and comforting me when I needed it, I developed an image of him in my mind that I know will come beautifully alive when I meet him face to face, either in heaven or when Jesus returns in glory.

This is the most precious gift Christ came to give us: eternal life. Since it's eternal, we don't have to wait to go to heaven to enjoy it because we already have it here through Jesus Christ who lives in us. Even though there have been days when I missed the dad I never met in the natural, I know that right now he is in the Cloud of Witnesses described in Hebrews 12:1 from where he is cheering us on, urging my siblings and me to run the race and to win it, just as he did!

I remember vividly the day I received Jesus at 12 years of age. From that moment on, I knew that I had eternal life and that death would not confine me to a cold grave. Instead, when I die, angels will take me into His presence where, after worshipping Him, I will finally be able to embrace my dad, who I'm sure will be wearing the crown that he sang about when he took his last breath on earth. Yes, Christ is our sure hope of glory because, "God so loved the world, that He gave His only begotten Son [Jesus], that whoever believes in Him shall not perish, but have eternal life" (John 3:16)!

If you don't have Jesus in your heart, I urge you to invite Him to save you right now because the Bible promises that, "As many as received Him, to them He gave the right to become children of God" (John 1:12). That is a blessing you shouldn't miss!

2 THE MOTHER WHO BROUGHT HEAVEN TO EARTH

"For the eyes of the Lord are toward the righteous, and His ears attend to their prayer..." (1 Peter 3:12)

When my father died, my mother had to take charge of the business. This was no small undertaking since my dad was a major developer of houses, and his company—the equivalent of Home Depot in the U.S.—sold everything that was needed to build a house, from materials for the foundation, to roofing and everything in between, including major appliances. His business also included a lumber mill and a quarry.

Quite unexpectedly my mother had to catch up with complex day-to-day operations that my dad had been handling before. It wasn't easy either, because in those days women were looked down on when it came to being in positions of leadership in the marketplace. But she had the Lord to lean on and she fully trusted Him in spite of the challenges at hand. Because of her strong faith, she didn't get bitter or angry with God. Instead, she consistently gave Him all the glory and honor for His love and faithfulness toward her and her children.

An excellent example of her unshakeable trust in God was an occasion when a major bill came due for the business. She combed through the ledgers looking for funds to pay it. She found an entry for someone who owed a sum similar to the impending bill, but since that person had left the country, she knew there was no way she could collect from him.

She began praying over the books when her unbelieving bookkeeper, who was watching from a distance, told her, "Señora, praying is okay, but if you don't pay by next Thursday, you are going to be in big trouble."

My mom firmly replied, "I have a big God who answers prayer."

He countered skeptically, "I don't know about that…" and left, shaking his head. Given the machismo prevalent in the country at the time, he may have also been muttering to himself, *Women belong in the kitchen, not in management.*

But on the day before the due date, there was a knock at the door and a man that my mom didn't recognize was standing there with a purposeful look on his face.

He said, "Good morning, Mrs. Palau. I'm so sorry to hear that your husband has passed away." He continued, "I am here to right a wrong. I left Argentina years ago owing people money that I couldn't pay. But while I was in Spain, I got back on my feet financially. Then someone told me about the love of God and His forgiveness, and today I am a new person. I received Jesus in my heart and I came back to repay everything, including what I owed your husband."

MY MOTHER, MATILDE BALFOUR PALAU

I can only imagine the joy my mother must have felt, and possibly the tears shed, when she received that payment because it was the amount she had been praying for. It was a powerful demonstration of God's provision!

She often told us this story and I never forgot it because it built my faith by reassuring me that we can always trust the Lord when facing humanly impossible situations.

Jesus is the same yesterday, today and forever, and nothing is impossible for Him. If you are facing a similar challenge today, the Lord can give you a miracle, and when He does, tell others about it, especially your children.

3 THE CHILDREN WHO CALL HER BLESSED

Due to the death of my father, my mother was forced to make adjustments to the comfortable lifestyle he had provided and to which she was accustomed. My sister Martha, who is seven years older than me, described it this way: "When our dad was alive, my mom had two nannies, several maids, a cook and a seamstress, in addition to a chauffeur, a gardener and a stable hand who took care of the horses the kids rode.[1]"

With my dad gone, this lifestyle was no longer sustainable, especially the hired help needed to care for so many children. She arranged for her three school age daughters to attend a British boarding school in the province of Cordoba, and my brother Luis was already a pupil at a similar school in a suburb of Buenos Aires. This allowed her to downsize and rent both the large house where she had lived with my dad, as well as an adjacent house, and move to a smaller one with my sister Margarita and I, the youngest of her brood.

Mother worked hard to keep the business afloat but the economy was not cooperating. This was compounded by the fact that the manager she hired had been cleverly stealing merchandise and cash[2], so eventually she rented all the properties and moved 300 miles away to Cordoba with me and Margarita to be closer to the other daughters who were in a boarding school in the hills nearby. She also found a nice church where we all grew up in faith and wonderful friendships. To supplement the income from the rental properties, she taught French, English and piano at home so she could be with us. What a caring and industrious mother!

Eventually, she met a very nice man and fell in love again. Pedro was a wonderful person. I was so excited that I was going to have a dad. He was very caring, always giving us lots of love and showering us with presents. I remember the time he built me a small wood bench, painted it green and named it "El Pampero," after the wind that sweeps the Argentine pampas. Why he chose that name, I have no idea, but I do recall him telling me, "This is your bench," and I proudly sat on my bench every day. This is the childhood gift that I remember most fondly.

During this time, my sister Margarita and I were the only ones living at home since the older ones were away at boarding schools. For us, the two youngest, Pedro was the

---

[1] Martha Palau Ortiz, *A Few Memoirs of Childhood and Early Adolescence* (Unpublished).
[2] Matilde Palau Dibble, *But Once* (Buenos Aires, Argentina: MAJESTAD Ediciones, July, 2007).

only dad we ever knew because he filled the vacuum left by the dad I never met, and Margarita was too young to remember. Then, Jorge was born. He was such a beautiful baby! Margarita and I, and all our siblings, were so happy to have such a cute and happy little brother. But tragedy struck again, and when Jorge was just nine months old, Pedro died of a heart attack. It was devastating for all of us.

The loss of Pedro, the freeze on rents imposed by the Peronist government that negatively impacted the revenue my mom got from the properties in Ingeniero Maschwitz, and the declining returns on my dad's business, all converged to put tremendous financial pressure on my mother. But she constantly reminded us of the promise in Romans 8:28, "God causes all things to work together for good to those who love God," and reassured us that He would see us through.

> She taught French, English and piano at home so she could be with us. What a caring and industrious mother!

After graduating from St. Alban College, my brother Luis was hired at the Bank of London in Buenos Aires, and after one year he transferred to its branch in Cordoba to be with us. My sister Matilde, once she finished her studies, also came home and worked as an executive secretary in an international corporation that valued her bilingual skills. I am sure that given Argentina's perennial feast-or-famine economy, those must have been very difficult financial times for the family. In fact, my brother Luis alluded to this in his recent biography[3].

But we, the younger ones, did not notice because my mother and our older siblings took good care of us, something for which I am most grateful. My sister Margarita and I had a British nanny who often took us to enjoy formal afternoon teas at a fancy hotel downtown, I attended William Morris (a private Christian school), and my brother was enrolled in a boarding school, so we did not feel deprived in any way.

Even though her father was a very prejudiced Scotsman, my mother had no social prejudices herself. She enjoyed having all kinds of people in our home. Her High Tea times with distinguished English ladies were legendary, but she also hosted young folks who were studying away from home (Cordoba being a university city), as well as the sick and the lonely.

Among the regulars was a paralytic woman that had to be carried home after each visit. A friend of my younger brother once complained to him, "I don't want to go to your house because you always have sick and poor people over!" But thanks to my mother's steadfast example, we knew we were doing the right thing.

---

[3] Luis Palau with Paul J. Pastor, *A Life on Fire: The Spiritual Memoir of Luis Palau* (Zondervan, 2019).

Mother was also fun to be around and the young people loved her for that, so much so that the youth in our church always included her in parties and celebrations. On Saturdays, she would take us to teach Bible stories to children in poor neighborhoods. We would play the guitar, sing Christian songs, and promise them candy to entice them to stay for the Bible lesson.

One day, someone we invited to come along asked me, "Why do we have to go and waste our time with poor malnourished kids who don't understand anything?" But my mom was undeterred because she believed that the seeds we were planting would bear good fruit.

Sure enough, many years after we had moved away from Cordoba we got a letter from a lady who wrote the following:

> *I finally found an address for the Palau family so I can thank you because your mother used to come to our slum to tell us about Jesus when I was little. She had so much love for us poor and rambunctious kids. I never forgot her, especially her sweet expression, even when we were being disrespectful. I am the one nicknamed "Marmalade." I was one of the worst behaved; I went just to get the candy. But a few years ago, I came to know Jesus personally. I am married now with kids of my own and my husband and I teach others about God like your mother did, and many are coming to Jesus.*

This woman saw Jesus in my mom and the result was fruit, much fruit, and fruit that remains and is being multiplied!

More than making an impact, my mother left a Jesus-shaped imprint on my siblings and me. As a result, her virtues and values are forever embedded in all of us.

> More than making an impact, my mother left a Jesus-shaped imprint on my siblings and me.

Her passion for winning souls is carried on by Luis. His devotion to personal evangelism is what Matilde has turned into a lifestyle. Martha inherited my mom's superb gift of hospitality. The home she built with her husband is the preferred gathering place for the family. Ketty exhibits extraordinary joy from helping others like my mom used to do, and Margarita has raised the largest number of children (seven, like my mom) with the same devotion and wisdom. My "baby brother" Jorge inherited her compassion for the needy and hurting which he displayed while serving the homeless in earlier years, and now in the California court system as a professional interpreter where he shines for Jesus.

LUIS MATILDE MARTHA KETTY

MARGARITA RUTH JORGE

He recently wrote me a letter that means so much to me:

To my sweet sister, the one with whom I shared things I didn't share with the others because of our closeness in age. Remember when we formed a "band" with the kids in the neighborhood? There are so many other things that would take too long to write about, but the time that sticks out in my memory was the year you spent in Cordoba before moving to San Nicolas. Your companionship helped me with my spiritual life…you taught me chords on the guitar and we sang together…and we talked often about the Lord and ministry. It was an unforgettable year! Thank you for sticking by me; you helped me to get strong in the Lord. I love you so much! Thanks for including me in your book. I love you and your family with all my heart. ~ George

Ed best described my mother when he said, "Like rose petals that are crushed to obtain a miniscule amount of nectar that produces a bottle of perfume, the aroma of Christ your mother emanated through the trials and challenges she overcame lives many times larger in all of you."

Very appropriately, Romans 8:28 was her favorite verse: "And we know that God causes all things to work together for good to those who love God, to those who are called according to His purpose." Deep down she knew that all things—good and bad, pretty and ugly, pleasant and unpleasant—would eventually work together for good. This was the secret that gave her the strength to persevere and be gracious under fire.

4 THE PHOTO THAT IGNITED A LIFELONG ROMANCE

When I was in my mid-teen years and living in Cordoba, someone came to visit and showed me a picture of his church's youth group in the city of San Nicolas. When I looked at it, I spontaneously said, "I like the tall, handsome one in the middle."

"Oh," he replied, "that one is the leader of our youth group. His name is Edgardo Silvoso."

Even though in that moment I felt "something" special deep inside—as if the Lord was telling me that he was "the one"—I kept my hopes in check because there was little chance of us ever meeting since we lived over 300 miles apart and attended churches that were not in fellowship with each other. In fact, they were at opposite poles theologically. What I didn't know, however, was that around the same time, my future brother-in-law (Miguel Angel Pujol) had shown Ed a picture of my family. He pointed to Margarita and told Ed, "This is my girlfriend with her family."

Ed later told me that when he looked at that picture, he felt the Lord telling him, "The girl in the lower right corner of the photo is the one I have prepared for you." He immediately asked for a magnifying glass to see the image more clearly. Why? Well, for the Millennials and younger generation that may be reading this story, unlike today, when we can enlarge photos on a smart phone screen with our fingers, back then they were printed on paper. This particular picture was a small black and white print with serrated edges.

After looking at the magnified image, Ed exclaimed, "Wow! Lord, you have good taste!" Right then he felt that I was the one for him. This was a much-awaited moment for Ed because after receiving Christ he decided that he would not date anyone until God showed him who the right girl was.

We had no way of connecting due to the geographic distance that separated us, but amazingly, a few months later my sister Martha made plans to be married in a civil ceremony in Ed's hometown. The reason for this was two-fold: first, in Argentina, churches do not have legal authority to perform marriages; that has to be done by a Justice of the Peace. The Church conducts the spiritual ceremony but not the one that is legally binding. The second reason was that her fiancé, Juan Carlos Ortiz, was working and

ministering in San Nicolas at the time, and after the civil ceremony they planned to have the marriage blessed in a church in Buenos Aires. So, my mom and I trekked to San Nicolas to be present at the civil ceremony, but I was also hoping to check out this "picture perfect" guy!

Prior to that trip, every time I came across someone who knew Ed, I mined that person for information. This is how I learned that his family was well respected in secular circles and that they were in leadership at their church. Finally, the day arrived, and the moment I saw him I liked him right away! It was definitely love at first sight! If a picture is worth a thousand words, a personal encounter is worth a whole library of books, not to mention a billion heartbeats!

I had never met such a committed and righteous young believer like Ed, and so good-looking—tall, elegant, articulate, educated, and an inspiring leader. I couldn't believe that such person existed. That night I asked my mom, "What is your impression of him?"

> The girl in the lower right corner of the photo is the one I have prepared for you.

She said, "He comes across as a fervent Christian, and like a British gentleman, too!"

That was a huge compliment coming from my mom because she was of British descent and the British are very proud of their lineage. Many years later, we learned that she had been right, because when we had our DNA testing done, the results confirmed that he has primarily Italian and English blood, along with some Spanish.

While in San Nicolas, I became close friends with his sister, Maria Rosa. Very astutely I invited her to come on holiday to Cordoba, aware that since she was only 12 at the time, she would need "someone"—most likely her brother—to accompany her.

As planned (or plotted, should I say?), the following summer Ed and his sister came "to visit my family." Actually, the family angle was the cover. We both knew that getting to know each other was the undeclared objective of the trip, and his sister was a blessed accessory, so to speak. The night before their arrival, I was so nervous that I didn't sleep at all. My mom and I went to pick them up at the bus station, and they stayed at our house where they met my sister Matilde and my younger brother Jorge. Both were taken by Ed and Maria Rosa's friendliness and enthusiasm about life in general, and the things of the Lord in particular.

It was evident that we liked each other, but we still hadn't expressed our feelings to each other.

After touring the city's landmarks for a few days, with my mom's permission we went to the hill country on holiday to stay with some family friends. The first day in the picturesque town of La Cumbre, we talked about every imaginable subject. We had so much fun! Ed loved to hear me play the guitar and sing. He told me my contralto voice was the sweetest he'd ever heard. I was mesmerized by how much he had done in life already as a student, a leader, and a developing entrepreneur. It was evident that we liked each other, but we still hadn't expressed our feelings to each other. But if eyes could talk…there was plenty that was being said already!

On our second day in the hills, we went for a walk and Ed led me to sit on a rock in the middle of a beautiful stream called El Chorrito, and he sat at my feet. I knew something was coming! He took my hands in his, looked me in the eyes and told me that he loved me and wanted to begin courting me. Would I agree? Absolutely! I readily accepted. It could not have happened in a more romantic setting!

That night he gave me a letter he had composed beforehand in which he wrote, "By the time you read this, we will be committed to each other. Even though I haven't told you about my feelings until now, I have known all along that you are the one that God has for me, and I sense that you feel the same way about me, too…"

After reading the letter, I asked him, "How did you know it was going to turn out this way?"

He replied with a smile, "I just knew it." Maybe he was a prophet…and a romantic one, too!

With the letter, he gave me an expensive bottle of perfume imported from Spain. Later on, I learned that he had spent a sizeable amount of his savings on it. When I brought this up, he simply said, "You are worth every drop and more…"

The rest of our vacation was spent hiking in the hills, swimming, horseback riding, preaching in churches, enriched by times of prayer and Bible reading and sharing our hopes and dreams. Maria Rosa was very discreet and allowed us to have plenty of time alone, but we made sure she did not feel excluded.

Upon our return to Cordoba, Ed asked my mom's permission to enter into courtship with me. My mother approved, and being the godly woman that she was, told us that she would be praying for the Lord to lead us every step of the way. How reassuring it was to know that we had her blessing and prayers as we embarked on this romantic journey, the first (and only) one for both of us. She also gave me permission to go with him and his sister to San Nicolas to share the news with Ed's parents and to seek their blessing. When we told them, they were elated and welcomed me like another daughter.

Our parents had all been praying for us to find the right spouse from the time we were very young. Their righteous lives led us to love God while growing up, and their service to Him impressed on us, from the very beginning of our courtship, that we would serve the Lord, too.

The Lord answered those prayers and He gave me the best husband in the world!

The most important decision a Christian makes—after receiving Jesus as their personal Savior—is choosing a life partner. If you are single, trust God to guide you. If you are a parent, pray for your children's future spouse and encourage them to pray, too. We did that with our daughters and God led each one of them to the husband they prayed for from the time they were little. He can do it for you, too!

5 THE ATHEIST WHO BECAME A PASTOR

Ed and his sister Maria Rosa grew up in a home with parents who gave them lots of love, attention, affirmation and confidence. They taught them to be honest and responsible.

Ed's mother, Teresa, was a devoted Catholic. His father, Omar—a strong and honest man—was loving, but in a quiet, manly way. He was a corporate executive and a vocational politician on the side. Unlike his wife, he was an atheist who enjoyed debating about religion until the day he met Jesus, at which time, like the Apostle Paul, he became an apologist for the Gospel. After serving as an elder in the church where he met the Lord, he planted a church that today is one of the largest in the region.

ED'S SISTER, MARIA ROSA

How did this family get to know Jesus? Well, God used a chief sinner to introduce them to God's forgiveness. This is how it happened.

One of Ed's uncles, a fun-loving but lost soul who never mentioned God except to use His name in vain, came to announce that God had radically changed his life. He told them about sick people being healed, drunkards delivered from alcohol, and marriages being restored at an evangelical church.

ED'S PARENTS, OMAR & TERESA

The Gospel was so new in San Nicolas that no one in the family had ever been to anything but a Catholic church. At first, they thought he was joking because if anyone was least likely to "catch religion," it was him. Nevertheless, he insisted that it was all real and invited them to go to one of the meetings to see for themselves.

The place he took them to wasn't a church building; it was a house where a businessman was telling people who had come from all over the city about Jesus. He had a compelling story to share because when his wife was dying, a preacher from the U.S. associated with the healing evangelist, Tommy Hicks, prayed for her and she was instantly healed. Shortly after, he got transferred to Ed's hometown where he and his wife started preaching the Gospel and praying for the sick with many people becoming evangelical Christians in a city that had never seen anything like that.

Ed, along with his mother and sister, went to see what had brought about such a change in his uncle. The first thing they heard was this well-known Gospel chorus:

At the Cross, at the Cross
Where I first saw the light
And the burdens of my heart rolled away.
It was there by faith I received my sight
And now I am happy all the time.

They had never heard lyrics like that in a church before, much less sung by common folks with such enthusiasm and fervor. It was contagious!

Next, someone opened the Bible to John 3:16, "For God so loved the world, that He gave His only begotten Son, that whoever believes in Him shall not perish, but have eternal life."

Ed told me later that they had never seen a Bible or heard that God loved sinners so much. They had been taught that God judged and punished sinners, not that He forgave so freely. They were blown away by the good news they were hearing for the first time. The preacher then turned to Isaiah 53:5, "He [Jesus] was pierced through for our transgressions, He was crushed for our iniquities; the chastening for our well-being fell upon him, and by his scourging we are healed." What a simple and still powerful and riveting presentation of the Gospel! To top it off, after the service the people embraced and kissed the newcomers. There was so much joy in that place!

Ed's mother, who had a disabling and very painful back condition, was healed instantly. She said, "Jesus forgave my sins and healed me all in one day." They went home rejoicing, full of excitement about what had happened.

Ed's dad, who was unaware of what they had experienced, saw his wife beaming with joy, and later noticed that she wasn't taking her pain medications. When he asked about it, she replied, "God healed me. Look! I can walk normally, like I used to."

He told her, "I don't know about God; in fact, I don't believe in God, but if you really are healed, I want to see what this is all about."

Soon afterward, he began to go to the meetings, but at first he stayed in the back, cautiously watching and listening, until finally one day he went forward to receive Christ as his Savior.

> Jesus forgave my sins and healed me all in one day... I can walk normally, like I used to.

It was a radical conversion, one that required some explanation given his public record as a consummate atheist, but Ed's dad never did anything half way. It was not enough for him to tell his relatives that he was no longer an atheist. He wanted to tell all his neighbors, too, since he had debated and, unfortunately, convinced some of them of the non-existence of God.

The opportunity came when the church decided to hold an open-air evangelistic meeting in his neighborhood. Ed's dad set the speakers up at the intersection, and before the preacher came to the microphone, he announced, "I want to apologize to all those I told before that God does not exist. I was wrong; He does. His son Jesus paid the price for our sins and now He lives in my heart. I am no longer an atheist. I am a Christian now and all my sins have been forgiven. If you would like to know more about this, come and see me." That day he led two neighbors to the Lord, and eventually he and Ed's mom would lead everyone in the neighborhood to Christ.

Supernatural joy came into the Silvoso home when Jesus came into their lives. God used a chief sinner to introduce the Gospel, which reminds us we should never despise small beginnings.

6 THE LADIES' MEETING THAT LAUNCHED A PREACHER

Within weeks of becoming a believer, Ed found himself in a most unusual situation, preaching at a ladies' meeting. Before I share the details, let me give you some background because what happened was truly remarkable.

At the time, Ed was studying (high school) while also working in a five-star hotel. He went to school from 7:00am to 1:00pm and worked from 4:00pm until midnight. This routine was not new to him because he had worked and studied simultaneously since elementary school; it was something he really wanted to do to contribute to the family budget, and his parents were not opposed because they believed it would build his character.

Ed was able to maintain this rigorous schedule because of his privileged mind. He can read very fast; he retains almost everything and can articulate the main points with unusual facility. All of that allowed him to always get good grades and be at the top of the class.

He had only one day off each week—Thursday. That was when he took a long nap to catch up on his lack of sleep. He would be so tired that he could have easily slept nonstop until the next day, but because Thursday was the only day of the week he could go to church, he always made a point to get up and go.

On one of those afternoons, while he was sound asleep, the Lord woke him up and instructed him very clearly to get up and go to a women's meeting in a slum area to preach to them.

That was a strange assignment because he didn't know what women did in those meetings, and he had never preached before. He had been a Christian for just a few months but wanted to be obedient to the voice of God. He knew the location because he had heard the announcement in church, so he got on his bike and took off.

The ladies' meeting took place inside a mud hut. He approached it hesitantly, and when he opened the door he found seven ladies praying, some of them with their face to the floor crying out to God. All of a sudden, one of them looked up and exclaimed joyfully, "Praise God! The servant of the Lord has arrived!"

Ed turned around to see who they were talking about, but no one else was there! He doesn't remember what he preached (most likely he shared his personal testimony), but the ladies were very blessed. Later that evening, Ed saw the pastor's wife, who was in charge of that meeting, and told her what had happened. Immediately she lifted her arms and exclaimed, "Praise the Lord! I couldn't go to preach today, so I asked the Lord to send another preacher… and I'm so glad to hear He did! Thank you for being obedient to the Lord."

He had been a Christian for just a few months but wanted to be obedient...

Her words about the Lord sending "a preacher" made a profound impact on Ed. He was a brand-new believer with no preaching experience, but the fact that the pastor's wife had prayed for a "preacher" to go and God had sent him planted the seed that made him the excellent communicator that he is today. Such is the power of positive Spirit-inspired words!

7 SEX OR A BLESSING

When Ed was leading the youth at the church, he taught them about holiness and how to keep themselves pure for their future spouse. In those days, parents didn't talk with their young people about sex, and even less about how to handle sexual temptations. The same was true for elders in the church. Sex was a taboo subject. Ed was a pioneer in that field. The youth group he led also organized social gatherings to which young non-believers were invited. This gradual approach was necessary because most unbelievers had never set foot inside an evangelical church. In fact, the Gospel was so unknown to the general public that all kinds of weird tales circulated about evangelicals. Opening the doors of the church in a social setting was a good way to debunk that, and often the visitors received the Lord.

One day, a new girl came to the social meeting. She was very attractive and appeared to be interested in the Gospel. She asked good questions and was very nice to everybody. At the end of the gathering she asked for somebody to take her home because it was dark outside and she lived far from there, alone with just her mother.

Ed asked the oldest boy, Jose, if he would do it, and he agreed. But when they got to the front of her house (which was on a dark street), the girl began to remove her blouse while enticing Jose to kiss her…and more! Startled, Jose asked, "Where is your mother? Aren't you afraid that she'll hear you?" She replied, "My mother can't hear anything because she's deaf." She persisted in trying to seduce him. "What's wrong? Am I not attractive to you?" And she proceeded to take off a more intimate piece of clothing.

Jose, filled with the Holy Spirit, opened the door of the house and went in to where the mother was seated watching the images on the TV screen with no sound obviously because she couldn't hear anything. He laid hands on her ears, prayed for God to touch her, and she was healed instantly! Jose then looked at the astonished daughter and said, "Do you see? I will never exchange this for that. Good night to you…and to your mother!"

The Scriptures tell us to "…worship the Lord in the beauty of holiness" (Psalm 96:9). When? Continuously. All the time, as a lifestyle. Why? Because holiness is beautiful. It draws us closer to God, and such intimacy makes temptations unappealing because what can compete with God? Jose was walking this young lady home "in the beauty of holiness," and because of that he was in position when God was ready to perform a miracle.

8 PRAYING LONG-DISTANCE

While we were courting, Ed and I lived and worked quite a distance from each other. In those days, neither one of us had a land-line phone, and there were no cell phones, so we wrote each other letters every week, but letters could take up to ten days to arrive. To compensate for that, we agreed to pray every night at 10:00 pm to be together "in the Spirit." I would pray in the hills of Cordoba and Ed would pray in San Nicolas.

During the summer months, his church would have evangelistic meetings every night and afterward the youth gathered at Ed's home. Argentines are night owls; they stay up late, so it was not uncommon that his friends would still be around when our prayer time came.

Eventually, they noticed that he would "disappear" around 10:00 pm for 15 to 30 minutes, and they asked him what he was doing. He told them, "I'm praying with my girlfriend."

"Can we join you?" they asked. Ed replied, "Since she isn't here, I don't mind. Sure!"

Every night, Ed and his friends prayed together, and soon they began to feel God's presence. As a result, those prayer times got longer and longer, first for an hour, then two, and eventually for most of the night. These young people were overflowing with joy. They quoted Scriptures, laid hands on each other, interceded for personal needs, confessed sins. Ed's bedroom became a miniature Upper Room saturated with the Holy Spirit. At one point, one of them said, "We must tell the pastor about this and ask his permission to go evangelize. We need to take Jesus to those who don't know Him yet!"

ED WITH ONE OF HIS EVANGELISTIC TEAMS

The pastor welcomed their desire to preach, even though most of them had no ministry experience. Nonetheless, he had them kneel down, laid hands on them, and sent them to evangelize three small towns nearby. They were so excited! Ed, at 18-years-old, was the lead evangelist; his associate was 16; his sister, the "music director," was 15; the youngest one, at 14, was the "youth leader," and the one they called "Grandpa" was 20.

> This was the start of a youth revival and the initiation into ministry for many of those kids.

With all the enthusiasm, faith and anointing the Lord bestowed on them, they spent two weekends in each one of those towns evangelizing. First, they went house-to-house distributing Gospel tracts, and later on, with an accordion and a portable PA system they carried on the bus, they sang at intersections to attract people's attention. Once they got a few to listen, they preached and invited them to receive Christ. Many came to Christ, even prostitutes and gang members. This was the start of a youth revival and the initiation into ministry for many of those kids.

I also felt the power of God in Los Cocos, the picturesque little village where I was teaching at a British boarding school. My prayer times also got longer and sweeter, and God deepened my desire to serve Him. Evidently, the Lord was preparing me for a future in ministry, too.

On Sundays (my day off), I began to teach Sunday School at a nearby church. Afterward, I helped the pastor by visiting those who hadn't come to the services. Because of his leadership position in the denomination he was a part of, he was called out of town quite often. When this happened, he would leave me in charge of the church. Even though I was young, I was still the most experienced because the rest were brand-new believers. I would pray and ask the Lord for help to do what I had not done before. I did everything: preaching, leading worship, taking the offering and giving the announcements. When I returned to Blair House (the boarding school where I taught), I was overflowing with the joy that comes from serving God on my day off work. It was all a part of my preparation for the ministry later on.

These experiences left a profound imprint on both of us because we felt the power and the presence of God flowing in and through us at a formative time in our lives. It all began when we made a commitment to pray every night. This is why small beginnings should never be despised.

It doesn't matter how small a first step is; if it leads you closer to God, take it and keep going because, "We are His workmanship, created in Christ Jesus for good works, which God prepared beforehand *so that we would walk in them*" (Ephesians 2:10, emphasis added).

9 TWO PRAYERS AND THE SERGEANT IN THE CROSSFIRE

Ed was drafted into the Army when he turned 20. It wasn't an easy transition for him after being in leadership positions in school, at work and in church. A new recruit is at the very bottom of the totem pole and those above him are not the kindest people. Many things happened during that time, but one incident in particular stands out.

There was a really mean-spirited drill sergeant who took exceptional gratification in putting the soldiers through as much torture as he could. He would have them do drills while beating them at the same time. He was often drunk and his wife was involved in demonic practices. He was not happy at home and he took his frustration out on the soldiers under his command in an abusive manner.

On Sundays, when relatives were allowed to visit the new recruits, he would put on a façade, smiling and singing with the guitar. But after people left, he would say, "Okay, soldiers, the show is over," and take up the torture once again. On cold nights, he would wake the entire company at 2:00 am and make everyone stand in their underwear on the parade grounds. He would go down the line, one by one, shouting and punching

ED IN ARMY UNIFORM

them. Those that he knocked down would be spit on and kicked. He took perverse pleasure in treating them this way.

Ed's mother was visiting him one Sunday, and when he saw the sergeant approaching, Ed immediately snapped to attention and saluted in the most perfect way because with that guy there was no room for even the most minimal error. After he passed by, Ed's mom told him, "That man needs the Lord. He looks so sad."

To that Ed replied, "Yes, but I am not the one who is going to tell him about the Lord. He is a mean and terrible man; he hates everyone, and especially evangelicals." In those days, evangelicals were few and far between and were considered a weird sect that deserved no respect, making them an easy target for bullying. Ed's mom said, "I am going to pray for you to be the one who witnesses to him." Ed was not very enthusiastic about that. In fact, he told me later that he felt like praying "against" it, but he knew better. He was no match for his mother when it came to prayer. But all the while, Ed was secretly hoping that someone else would be the answer to her prayers for the sergeant.

> Ed's mom said, "I am going to pray for *you* to be the one who witnesses to him."

A few days later, their paths crossed and Sergeant Gonzales barked, "Silvoso, get to my office on the double!"

Ed was concerned, not knowing what to expect. At best it would be a tongue lashing, at worst a beating. When he got there, Sergeant Gonzales opened a cabinet, took out a Bible and slammed it on the desk. "What do you think about this book?"

Ed didn't know if he was mocking him or trying to get him punished because, at that time in Argentina, military personnel had to be Catholic and reading the Bible was discouraged.

"Some nuns gave it to me," he added.

Ed realized this could be his opportunity to witness to this hardened and lost soul. Knowing that he might be stepping into a trap, he muttered a silent prayer for courage and wisdom and then explained, "That book is the Word of God. God wants to speak to you through its pages. You should read it."

The sergeant held a cold stare that revealed nothing for a long time. Then he said, "It is a big book. Where do I begin?"

Ed suggested the Gospel of John and opened the book to Chapter 1. The cold eyes returned, followed by another long stare. Ed felt like a deer in the sights of a hunter but did not let his fear show. Abruptly, the sergeant shouted, "You are dismissed! Get out of here!"

More than happy to oblige, Ed made a hasty exit, saying to himself, "At least I planted the seed. Now the rest is up to God. But I sure hope He does not send me to water it!"

All of this happened on a Friday. The following Monday, Ed noticed the sergeant approaching with red eyes and a puffy face. He thought, "Oh no! It's not even 8:00 am and he is already drunk. I better steer clear of him." But before he could, the sergeant ordered him to come to his office—on the double, of course. He told Ed to shut the door, and asked, "What is happening to me? I am a tough, macho guy, not a crybaby, but every time I come across the word Jesus in this book, I break down crying. Why?"

What is happening to me? I am a tough, macho guy, not a crybaby, but every time I come across the word Jesus, I break down.

Ed explained that God was leading him to Jesus for his sins to be forgiven. He quoted Revelation 3:20 to explain that Jesus was there with him, in that room, knocking at the door of his heart. If he would open it, Jesus would come in and make him a new person.

Showing genuine interest, he asked, "How do I do that?"

Ed offered to lead him in the sinner's prayer. He accepted and right there he received the Lord. The change was instantaneous. First, he cried uncontrollably, but those were cleansing tears washing the bad stuff out of him. When he stopped, his eyes and his smile were different. He was experiencing the miracle of being born again. Next, he stood up and embraced Ed, who must have been the first soldier ever to be hugged by this tough guy!

That was the week the sergeant was in charge of the commando company where Ed served. He supervised its activities during the day and slept in the barracks with them at night. Those were the evenings the soldiers dreaded the most because of his perverse habit of beating them in the middle of the night on the parade grounds. Ed suggested that they go to the church his father pastored that evening. The sergeant accepted, but later on, as they walked toward the gate, his drinking buddies insisted that he have a drink with them. Walking alongside him, Ed prayed fervently for the Lord to intervene. Turning down a drink from a friend, especially in the military, was usually perceived as a put down, or worse yet, as a sign of weakness. "So, you can't hold your liquor?"

The sergeant, being an alcoholic, was in a vulnerable position. Three times he was stopped and three times he was able to withstand it. Ed was thanking the Lord for those tiny breakthroughs. When they finally walked into the meeting, the congregation was singing, "I am a soldier of Jesus, a servant of the Lord. I will not fear to carry His cross, suffering for His sake." Only God could have orchestrated it. The sergeant had a powerful tenor voice. Ed got him a hymn book and he joined in, *standing at full attention!* Later on, he went forward and made a public confession of faith in Jesus.

But the real test was waiting back at the army base where evil was entrenched and his drinking buddies would be on the prowl. Ed was praying for a breakthrough and God heard him. When they arrived, his friends were not around and the soldiers were already in bed. The sergeant commanded the company to get out of bed and to stand to attention on the parade grounds. Everyone was bracing for the usual beating. Instead, what happened next was truly remarkable.

"At ease," he ordered, and then proceeded to tell them, "You have known me as the cruel, beating-driven sergeant, but from now on you will know me as the praying sergeant.

I have received Jesus in my heart and I am a new person. If you want to know more about it, come by my room (which was next to the soldiers' dormitory) and I will explain further." Then he said to Ed, "You stay with me to help with the explaining!"

That night, many soldiers were led to Christ. The rest of the week was unusually good for the soldiers who also heard the sergeant singing Christian songs. Ed became very popular with his fellow soldiers. Some bought him lunch as an expression of gratitude, and others came with suggestions like, "Could you also change that other sergeant?"

SERGEANT GONZALES

Many of those soldiers came to the Lord through the sergeant who openly witnessed about his new evangelical faith, but he was treading on thin ice because proselytizing was a punishable offense. The lieutenant colonel in charge of the base heard about what was going on and summoned Gonzales to deliver a threat, "Have you forgotten that military personnel are to be Catholics? If you don't stop talking about the Gospel, we will transfer you to Patagonia where you will freeze with the penguins and will never see a promotion. Stop proselytizing or else!"

> I have received Jesus in my heart and I am a new person. If you want to know more about it, come by my room.

Gonzales, standing at attention, responded, "A few months ago you threatened to send me there for always being drunk, and today, because I talk about the God who changed me, you are going to punish me? Very respectfully, Sir, may I ask, what is worse: to be a drunkard or a believer in Jesus?"

The logic was unbeatable and it completely disarmed the lieutenant coronel! The sergeant wasn't transferred, and before long everyone at the base had heard the Gospel because, in addition to the daily witnessing by the sergeant, by Ed and the new converts, Ed gave the farewell address at the discharge ceremony. He inserted a clear presentation of the Gospel and an invitation to hold God's hand through Jesus Christ into a speech that was laced with the usual patriotic metaphors and call to love and serve the motherland that every military person loves to hear.

What a powerful demonstration that the prayers of a mother and the obedience of a son, albeit reluctant at first, can work wonders.

10 THE POWER OF INTEGRITY

We live in a world where wrong is right and right is wrong, according to secular standards. Christians have a different moral code. How can a believer not just survive, but also thrive when the rules are so perverted?

The answer is found first in the Scriptures where we are instructed how to overcome evil. The apostle John, who was known for his clean heart and had to face the wrath of the Roman Emperor, wrote, "Greater is He who is in you than he who is in the world" (1 John 4:4).

When Ed was an up-and-coming young executive working in a very ungodly environment, he was able to experience and exercise the power of integrity.

He was on the fast-track for a top management position at an international hotel in Argentina. He lived an exemplary life that was tested time and again due to the prevailing corruption in business. One of those occasions was when the CEO instructed everybody to overcharge American customers when they placed a long distance call. This was easy to do because in those days international calls had to be placed through an operator, and their length, and cost to the customer, was not determined electronically like it is nowadays.

When Ed took the first request for a call, everybody's eyes were on him, wondering if he would compromise his standards. When asked what he would do, Ed replied that he would charge the correct amount. His coworkers reminded him that the boss wouldn't like that and, worse yet, that his advancement would be placed in jeopardy. Furthermore, a female employee (who was also the boss' mistress) put her index finger under Ed's chin and asked, "What are you going to do now, Mr. Saint?"

Ed reiterated his determination not to overcharge the customer, to which she purred sneeringly, " Then I'll just have to tell him."

Sure enough, not long afterward, his boss burst into Ed's office and, pointing a menacing finger and using the most vile language, proceeded to insult him in front of everybody. Ed was shocked but this did not prevent him from quietly praying for the Holy Spirit to assist him as he had read in the Scriptures. And He did!

> The Holy Spirit put the answer in Ed's mouth without him thinking about it.

When the boss asked through clenched teeth, "Why did you disobey me? Are you aware of the consequences?" The Holy Spirit put the answer in Ed's mouth without him thinking about it.

"Sir, if I am willing to risk my employment and advancement by refusing to cheat a gringo who will never know what I did for him, do you realize the certainty you can have that I will never steal from you?

The logic was absolutely disarming. There was nothing he could say. He snorted, turned around and slammed the door behind him. Everybody wondered what was going to happen next, and what took place was a modern-day enactment of Psalm 23:6. The Lord set a banqueting table in the presence of Ed's enemies when three hours later the boss had dinner for the two of them delivered to the same office where he had insulted Ed so cruelly. He made no reference to the incident, but that was his way of apologizing. Shortly afterward, Ed was promoted to be the second in command in the corporation, not unlike the case of Mordecai in the book of Esther.

Jesus assured his disciples on the eve of his arrest and cruxifion that he would not leave them as orphans (see John 14:18) because the Father was going to send the Holy Spirit to be with them and in them. Whatever evil challenge you are facing today, take hold of that truth and overcome evil with good!

THIS IS THE HOTEL WHERE ED WORKED AT THE TIME.

11 THE DAY GOD SPOKE IN THE BOARDROOM

After a wonderful seven-year courtship, we got married and had the most beautiful wedding imaginable. The ceremony was at the church that Ed's father had planted and was still pastoring. So many people came that the crowd overflowed all the way to the street. In fact, the mayor deployed additional personnel for traffic control. Since my dad had died, my uncle Arnoldo walked me down the aisle and my brother-in-law Juan Carlos Ortiz officiated.

There was a tangible presence of God throughout the ceremony and the unbelievers received a powerful witness. For those in the social upper class, it was their first time inside an evangelical church. And they loved it! Not the building, which could never have competed with the Catholic Cathedral where they went to mass, but the spiritual climate and the joy that the believers exuded. It was contagious.

The wedding reception took place at the nice hotel where Ed used to work. His former boss paid for it in appreciation of Ed's services. In fact, he told me very ceremoniously, "You are marrying a man of unsurpassed integrity." I suspect he was remembering the day Ed refused to cheat guests who made international calls.

When we returned from our honeymoon, the brand-new home we had built during our courtship was waiting for us. It was a three-bedroom house with a yard, furnished and nicely decorated. We were very much in love and happy to be married.

Ed was the CEO of a private hospital and sat on the board of directors of a bank, in addition to running an investment fund on the side. He has always been an excellent multitasker. On weekends we served the Lord—teaching Sunday School at the church, doing street evangelism, youth work, and more—with great joy. On Saturday mornings we often packed a picnic basket and went to a nearby ranch to ride horses and pray by the river that ran through the property.

Ed was making very good wages. We had a car and a house paid in full, which was unusual for a young couple. We enjoyed a comfortable lifestyle. During one of those prayer times at the ranch, we sensed the Lord impressing on us that He was going to use us in a more powerful way. We consecrated our lives to Him and began to seek God's guidance. We had had a similar experience at a youth camp before, so this was a confirmation.

> Whenever he didn't know how to deal with a situation, he would kneel in front of that chair and ask Jesus what to do.

Ed was doing great at the hospital, he enjoyed his job, and his reputation as an enterprising CEO had spread all over the region. Some days were very challenging because corruption was rampant, but we were committed to walk in integrity. There were no other believers in high positions in the marketplace that Ed could go to for mentoring, so he set aside a red chair in his office and called it "the Jesus chair," a place for the Lord to reside. Whenever he didn't know how to deal with a situation, he would kneel in front of that chair and ask Jesus for guidance. The Lord always answered those prayers and blessed his work to the pleasure of the board of directors.

One day soon after Ed had been instrumental in fencing off a hostile takeover, the board informed him that his salary was going to be doubled. He was honored, but at that precise moment he felt God telling him that it was time to go into the so-called "full-time ministry."

We were already ministering in the marketplace, witnessing to influential people including doctors and their wives. We were also busy doing church work, but evidently God was telling Ed that there was something more.

On the way home, Ed was wondering how he was going to tell me about leaving the hospital, the bank, and the investment fund he managed, to go into "church work," which was notorious for its low pay. What he didn't know was that during my morning prayers, the Lord had also shown me that we should move on. I didn't understand it at the time, and I was also wondering how Ed would respond in light of how well he was doing at work.

Ed told me about the huge salary raise first, and then about the Lord's message. I told him what the Lord had told me that morning. Immediately we started praising the Lord, overflowing with joy for such divine confirmation!

The board of directors was surprised and disappointed when Ed notified them that he was leaving. Thinking he had been offered a better paying position elsewhere, the doctors (behind Ed's back) asked me how much the "others" were offering so they could double it! I told them they'd never be able to match the other offer because it had eternal returns (even if not material). In fact, the salary in the church we ended up pastoring was nine times lower.

We were young and inexperienced, but we knew that God was with us and He had sent us there.

We didn't know where God would lead us, but we prayed for clarity. A week later, a congregation in the beautiful city of Mar del Plata, which means silver sea, contacted us to become their pastors. We agreed to take the position, rented out our house, and left with great joy in our hearts with our little baby girl Karina in the backseat of our car.

The church had the most beautiful building in the denomination at the time, donated by Kathryn Kuhlman, but it also had serious internal divisions. We were young and inexperienced, but we knew that God was with us and He had sent us there.

He gave us the necessary wisdom to deal with those challenges, not without tears and times of prayer crying out to God for insight, and especially for patience. And in the process, we learned how important it is to pastor people that are not always appreciative of the price their shepherds pay to care for them.

By the time we moved on, those divisions had been healed and a new batch of leaders was in place. Evidently, all things—pleasant and unpleasant as my mother used to say—work together for good.

12 THE BLESSINGS FROM CANADA

Ernest and Kathy Kerr, a marvelous missionary couple from Canada, became our spiritual parents in Argentina. They ministered at youth retreats that we faithfully attended while we were still teenagers. During a Bible study on faith and obedience that they taught, they looked at us and proclaimed, "One day you will reach an entire city for Christ." Humanly speaking, that was an incredible prediction because, in those days, churches were very small, evangelicals were second-class citizens, and an entire city had never been reached for Christ. But they spoke those words under the inspiration of the Holy Spirit and eventually it happened! And when it did, we remembered the seed they had planted many years earlier.

The Kerrs were also my favorite teachers at the Bible Institute in Buenos Aires where I studied while Ed was in the Army. They are the ones that helped us discern God's will when we felt led to leave the business world to go into the pastorate. At the time, they were pastoring the church in Mar del Plata that we were called to take over for them to return to Canada. During the transition they spent precious time teaching us the essentials of the pastorate.

As true spiritual parents, they always kept in touch, praying for us, sending us encouraging notes, and when we were studying in Portland they drove all the way from Canada to see us. It was a marvelous visit with rich times of prayer, fellowship and wise counsel.

During their stay, they invited us to speak at a missionary conference for the Pentecostal Assemblies of Canada (PAOC), the denomination they served under. I wasn't able to go because I was pregnant with Marilyn, so Ed went by himself. He had a great time in Vancouver, Canada, sharing from the pulpit, unaware that a powerful seed was being planted (thanks to the Kerrs) that later on would produce tremendous fruit all over the world.

THE KERRS WITH RUTH AND KARINA IN OREGON

This is how it came about: Ed stayed in the home of an elderly couple and the Kerrs decided to organize a meeting there for him to share our vision to evangelize Argentina. It was a small gathering, everybody was inspired by Ed's message, but we didn't think much about it at the time since the main objective for Ed's visit was to speak at the church. However, some time later, we received a very official looking letter from a lawyer in Canada notifying us that the elderly couple had passed away and named Ed as a beneficiary in their will. The timing

THE KERRS IN MAR DEL PLATA

could not have been more providential because that is the money we used to buy the land where eventually we built the chapel and the retreat center that became the point of inception for our current ministry.

In time, Ernest and Kathy Kerr also went to be with the Lord. At the time of his death, Ernest was ministering at a camp and while watching a group of young people praying, he began to sing, "The Earth is Full of His Glory," and halfway through it he was taken into the fullness of His presence in heaven.

Kathy lived longer and we were able to take her to one of our conferences in Mar del Plata to see the fruit of their missionary work in Argentina. The day before her promotion to heaven, she told her caretaker, "Write to Ed and Ruth and send them my love." What a dramatic passing of the baton! I can picture the Kerrs in the Cloud of Witnesses, along with the other Canadian couple, urging us to run the race. We are so grateful to Canada for having sent missionaries who mentored us and introduced us to other Canadians who empowered us to build a chapel from where transformation has spread to every continent.

Back then, what we saw was a wonderful friendship and mentoring relationship, but God had much more in mind. This is a reminder that we can count the seeds in an apple, but only God can count the apples in each seed. What is before your eyes is only a fraction of the "much more" that God has in store for you (see 2 Corinthians 3:9).

13 THE LORD IS OUR PROVIDER

After pastoring in Mar del Plata, the Lord made a way for us to move to Mexico, thanks to the kindness of my brother Luis and his wife Pat, who provided the funds and invited us to join their evangelistic team there. Later on, they made it possible for us to go to the U.S. to study in Portland, Oregon. Ed enrolled in the grad course at Multnomah School of the Bible (now Multnomah University) and I took night classes because I was already pregnant with Marilyn.

Since we came straight from pastoring, where the salary was meager, we had no savings. In order to support ourselves, Ed (the consummate multitasker) earned some money answering the myriad of letters that came in response to Luis' radio programs, worked part-time at a gas station, and played soccer for the school in exchange for a scholarship. I babysat for some of our fellow students.

Our budget was and felt very tight when compared to how comfortably we lived in San Nicolas. It wasn't easy, but we were glad to be studying the Bible in the U.S. When my birthday came, Ed decided to surprise me by cooking a special breakfast. He went to the store to buy something that was more expensive than our usual groceries, but when he got to the cashier, he realized that he didn't have enough money. He was very embarrassed, put the food back on the shelf, walked home, and fixed the usual breakfast.

We had a good time playing with our "baby" Karina, but I could tell that Ed was sad even though he managed to put up a good front. He was also concerned because we had no medical insurance to

MULTNOMAH PRAYER CHAPEL

cover the delivery of the new baby. To challenge our faith further, registration for the next semester was coming up. We prayed and put everything in the Lord's hands.

The next day, when Ed went to the school post office to pick up the mail, he found an envelope addressed to us and stuffed with brand new dollar bills and this note inside:

"We are so glad that you came to the U.S. because you are such a blessing to us and to many others. This is a gift for you. Use it as needed. We won't tell you who we are so that any time you see an American, you will wonder if perhaps he or she is the one who blessed you with this gift."

And inside the envelope there was plenty of money to cover all our needs and more!

When Ed showed it to me, I remembered the story of when my mom was short on money to pay a pressing bill, and that stranger came back from Spain to cancel a debt that matched what she needed. God is faithful and totally committed to our welfare. If you have any doubts, look around and remember this verse: "Look at the birds of the air, that they do not sow, nor reap nor gather into barns, and yet your heavenly Father feeds them. Are you not worth much more than they?" (Matthew 6:26)

14 THE LEUKEMIA THAT VANISHED

After Portland, we moved to Southern California for further training. While Ed was studying at Fuller Theological Seminary in Pasadena, I enrolled in Charm School in nearby Glendale just for fun. Later on, I studied Interior Decorating and Design, something that I enjoyed immensely. It was so fun and exciting to learn how to present things in the best possible light for people to enjoy them. I believe God is the Supreme Interior and Exterior Decorator, not only because of the beautiful way He arranged the heavens and the earth, but also through the designs He gave to Moses for the Tabernacle and to Solomon for the Temple. It's breathtaking to see the colors, the materials, the jewels, the fine woods and the craftsmanship He chose. His tastes were and still are exquisite!

It was right after our studies in California that we returned to Argentina. We were so excited to be back to serve the Lord by opening an office for the Palau Evangelistic Association and setting up evangelistic crusades for my brother Luis.

But shortly after arriving, I started to feel very weak and began to lose weight at an alarming rate. Something was definitely wrong, so I was admitted to the British Hospital in Buenos Aires. We were still house hunting and had all our things in suitcases and boxes. It was a challenging situation, so my sisters helped take care of our girls while I was hospitalized.

After many tests, the doctors determined that the diagnosis was Leukemia. As was customary in those days, they didn't tell the patient when a prognosis was that bad, but instead spoke to the next of kin; in this case, Ed. He was stunned by the dreadful news. We were eager to go all out for the Lord and now he was confronted with the prospect of losing me.

In order to focus on something positive—typical for Ed when facing a negative—he decided to do street evangelism in the evenings when the hospital did not allow visitors.

He rented a portable electric generator and a sound system and every night he stood in the middle of Plaza Once—a very busy intersection in Buenos Aires where bus, subway and train lines converge, ensuring a large crowd—telling people about Jesus. He thought, *I believe God for the best, but if He decides to take Ruth, I am going to take a few with me to heaven. Satan is not going to win now, or ever. We came here to preach the Gospel, and the Gospel, which is the power of God, shall be preached.*

Upon hearing the news of my diagnosis, an elder from the church we had pastored in Mar del Plata assured Ed, "We are going to have a vigil and pray for Ruth all night until she is healed."

> We came here to preach the Gospel, and the Gospel, which is the power of God, shall be preached.

Ed needed that level of encouragement because every day he came to visit me, he saw how much worse I looked. I was very pale and increasingly feeble, I couldn't hold down food and I continued to lose weight.

A week later, this elder, who understood spiritual warfare and intercession better than we did at the time, called Ed very early one morning and told him, "It is done."

Ed asked, "*What* is done?"

Matter-of-factly, he replied, "She is healed. Go to the hospital and you will see."

When Ed arrived, he was instructed to stop at the doctor's office. There, a very chagrinned doctor told him, "We owe you a huge apology."

Ed asked why, and she continued, "We misdiagnosed your wife. Based on the original tests, we were convinced that she had Leukemia, but we have repeated those tests for two days in a row and they now show that she does not have Leukemia. In fact, she is free of any disease. Would you please accept our apology?"

Ed reassured her that no apologies were necessary because God had performed a miracle. This, in turn, allowed the doctor to come closer to the Kingdom of God even if she did not receive the Lord right then.

"I, the Lord, am your healer" (Exodus 15:26) is a promise guaranteed by Jesus' stripes because by His wounds we were healed (Isaiah 53:5). Yes, God is our healer. Take a moment now to pray for someone who is ill and pray a prayer of faith. A prayer of faith is a prayer uttered standing on the Word of God and claiming its promises in the Name that is above all names, Jesus, the One who has all authority in heaven and on earth. He is able. Let us never stop praying those prayers.

ED DOING STREET EVANGELISM

15 THE NIGHT THE ARGENTINE DIRTY WAR CAME KNOCKING

The Argentine military launched an all-out war against leftist urban guerrillas. It was so brutal that it came to be known as "the dirty war." Both sides killed each other mercilessly. Many young people, subversives or sympathetic to their cause, would be arrested, usually in the middle of the night when no one was around, and taken to a secret government detention center where they were tortured and eventually killed. These people are referred to as "Los Desaparecidos," or "The Missing Ones."

It was right in the middle of this terrifying time that we settled in Rosario to launch the Luis Palau ministry in Argentina. This city was one of the main centers of rebellion and repression and people were killed every week, sometimes every day.

Sadly, many of Ed's classmates from high school had become "guerilla fighters," inspired by Che Guevara and Fidel Castro. Some of these misguided idealists were among those who disappeared. That made Ed suspect in the eyes of the Army since he had gone to school with them. The fact that he had served in the Army in a commando company made him a target for the guerrillas. We were caught between two groups bent on killing each other and anyone they merely suspected, ourselves included.

Ed was busily visiting pastors in the region to encourage them to come together in unity for the upcoming crusade that he was coordinating for my brother. That meant that he had a lot of visibility and often came home late at night.

Those were dangerous days. The first day we moved into our house, when we were putting the girls to bed, machine gunfire broke out across the street. Bullets flew in every direction. Ed and I jumped on top of our girls to protect them with our bodies. That was not the only time; many nights there were shootings all over the city, and bombs went off continually. In the morning, we would learn of the casualties. The shedding of blood became so common that people got used to asking, "How many were killed last night?" as if asking if it had rained the night before. Murder and death became a part of life. How sad!

One night, when I was pregnant with our third daughter Evelyn, Ed had gone to another city for a pre-crusade meeting and I was home alone with our two girls. We didn't have a phone in the house and it was late.

> Murder and death became a part of life. How sad!

When the doorbell kept ringing insistently, I looked from the balcony on the second floor to see who was calling so late since I was not expecting anyone. Besides, people did not venture out at night due to the violence. At the door, I saw a man I didn't recognize and several others inside the car he'd arrived in. From the window I asked him what he wanted, and he said, "We are waiting for your husband."

I told him, "They'll be coming back soon" (in reality, Ed was by himself but since God was with him, I said "they," hoping to impress on him that Ed was not alone).

He replied coldly, "We know he's not here but we'll wait until he returns. We have business with him." Business often meant you could become another desaparecido since they were taking captives at night when there was no one else around.

I started shaking because I suspected they had come to do just that. In those days you wouldn't know if it was the army or the guerillas calling because the latter would steal army uniforms and dress like soldiers. On the other hand, there was a huge number of undercover policemen and intelligence officers who dressed in civilian clothes. You couldn't trust anyone.

This man and his three companions waited outside for hours. Every time I opened a window to spy, they were there. I could also smell the smoke of their cigarettes which told me they were most likely not believers. I prayed and prayed for protection until, exhausted, I fell asleep on my knees by our bed.

I was rudely awakened at 4:00 am by the sound of doors opening and closing. I had locked all the interior doors (a total of seven between the main entrance and our bedroom) and barricaded myself in the bedroom with our two girls. I could hear footsteps, and then someone trying to open our bedroom door. This is it, I thought. They got Ed and now they are coming for me and the girls.

To my relief, when I peeked through the keyhole I saw that it was Ed! He had returned home and was confused because he didn't understand why I had locked all the doors and was holed up in the bedroom. I let him in and explained what had happened that night.

He then told me that the car had broken down in a remote area and he had to walk a long distance for help in the middle of the night. There were no cell phones in those days, and road assistance was not available! It took him hours to find help, but that is what spared him. Praise God for divinely orchestrated car trouble!

We thanked God that He allowed that to happen to protect us because those men eventually tired of waiting and left! As scary as this experience was, it did not deter us from continuing to minister and to organize my brother's crusade. What looked like a major mechanical problem for Ed, turned out to be divine intervention to protect us at home. What a wonderful God we serve!

16 THE HOLY SPIRIT AVERTING A KIDNAP

No matter how brave we think we are, when danger or tragedy touches our children, we feel very vulnerable because those under our care have been violated and we sense that we have failed to protect them. That's the way I felt the day our oldest daughter, Karina, became the target of a kidnap attempt. Kidnaps for ransom or for sexual exploitation had become more common in those days since the police had stopped patrolling due to fear of being killed by guerillas who would then take their weapons.

Karina, eight-years-old at the time, was enrolled at the Latin American School in downtown Rosario. The school was originally called "The American School," but the leftist guerrillas threatened to bomb it unless they dropped the word "American." Such was the brutal political climate. Classes were taught in Spanish in the morning and in English in the afternoon. In between, she came home for lunch. We had hired someone to take her to school and bring her home when Ed couldn't drive her. On that particular day, Ed was far away in Resistencia. She was ready to be taken back to school when I felt uneasy about sending her with that person. In fact, it was a strong warning, which I knew came from God because it did not scare me. It just made me aware that danger was lurking. The Holy Spirit was speaking to me quietly, but clearly, so I told Ed's secretary, who was there that day, that she should take her instead.

With Ed gone, they would have to catch the city bus a block away. As they walked down the street hand in hand, they saw a mean-looking man get out of a car where three other sinister characters were seated. Karina later told us that while they walked, the Holy Spirit was speaking to her in an almost audible voice, telling her, "Turn around and run home now!"

> ...it was a strong warning, which I knew came from God...

She tried to tell Ed's secretary that she had to go back home, but she wouldn't listen, so Karina broke free and started running toward the house as she chased after her. They barely made it home, bursting through the door just in time to avoid the men that had been waiting to snatch Karina, overcome with shock. When they told me what had happened, I realized that we could have lost our beloved daughter to a band of criminals that may have still been waiting outside. I felt so vulnerable!

Ed was in Resistencia that day to host and coordinate the ministry of a Christian basketball team from what is now William Jessup University. They would play local teams, pass out Gospel tracts and share testimonies during half-time. Seven hours before the kidnap attempt, the Holy Spirit awakened Ed and instructed him to drive home as fast as he dared. He told his assistant to take charge and with a growing sense of urgency he took off.

Ed fully enjoyed the thrill of driving fast, which in those days was an offense the police never pulled you over for. It was a macho and cultural thing, especially since one of our national heroes, Juan Manuel Fangio, was the first Formula One racer to win the World Championship five times.

Ed covered the 500 plus miles in less than six hours, praying all the way. In those days, there was no phone connection available, so he had no way of knowing what was going on. All he sensed was that our beloved daughter Karina was in danger. He entered the city at about the time that Karina was due to arrive at school for afternoon classes. He asked the Holy Spirit if he should go there or home instead. "Home!" He said.

By then, the person assigned to take Karina had confessed that he had agreed to deliver her to the kidnappers because they had threatened him with death if he didn't. I was in a very vulnerable position when, all of a sudden, I saw Ed pulling into the driveway. When he learned what had happened, he took control of the situation, dismissed the man, took away his keys to our house and warned him sternly to never come back.

What could have been an irreparable tragedy for our family, and a life-long trauma for Karina, was totally averted because the Holy Spirit, faithful to His nature, warned us and led us to safety. It also solidified for Karina, even at such a young age, the realization that she knew God's voice—what it sounded like—and that it could be trusted. She didn't hesitate to obey without question when the Holy Spirit told her to run. Having been raised in a home where prayer was as natural as talking and breathing, it wasn't hard to hear God's voice as she did in this instance. She and her husband Gary have done the same with their children. What a blessing!

Remember that His promise is that He will never leave you, nor forsake you. Never! (See Joshua 1:5 NIV)

KARINA GREW UP TO BECOME A
STRONG AND WISE LEADER. TODAY, SHE
AND HER HUSBAND GARY, AND THEIR
FOUR CHILDREN (VANESSA, SOPHIA,
ISABELLA AND NATHAN) LOVE AND
SERVE THE LORD AS A FAMILY.

17 ANGELS PROVIDING ROAD ASSISTANCE

For He will give His angels charge concerning you,
to guard you in all your ways. (Psalm 91:11)

We are very aware that Jesus lives in our heart, the Holy Spirit is ready to guide us, and the Father loves us dearly. Those truths related to the ministry of the Trinity are very familiar and comforting to us. However, we need to see with the same clarity that angels are also involved in ministry to humans when it comes to guarding and guiding us.

When our two daughters, Karina and Marilyn, were five and eight-years old, we traveled by car from Argentina to Brazil to share about what we were doing there to combine discipleship with crusade evangelism since it was a new approach. It was a three-day drive from Rosario (where we lived) to São Paulo. We drove the first day without any problems. The second day we stopped for dinner after 11 hours on the road, with Ed having done all the driving since his style was a good match for the equally aggressive Brazilians on the road!

As we were savoring an excellent Brazilian after-dinner coffee, we studied the paper road map (there was no GPS in those days), debating whether to continue to the next big city (Curitiba) or to stay in that small town overnight. Even though it had been a long day and fatigue was setting in, we decided to press on. We estimated that it would take two hours at the most to get there. Even though we were tired, the highway had been in good condition, so we figured we could do it and reward ourselves by sleeping more comfortably in a big city.

Although there were thick clouds threatening a storm, we prayed and off we went singing a song that went like this:

I just keep trusting my Lord as I walk along
I just keep trusting my Lord and He gives a song
Though the storm clouds darken the sky o'er the heav'nly trail
I just keep trusting my Lord, He will never fail
He's a faithful friend, such a faithful friend
I can count on Him to the very end
Though the storm clouds darken the sky o'er the heav'nly trail
I just keep trusting my Lord, He will never fail

We soon found out that the wide highway we had been driving on all day turned into a narrow two-lane winding mountain road with no shoulders. On one side was a hill and on the other a precipice. It was almost dark, the fog was rolling in, and it began to rain. To compound matters, there was no place to pull over or turn around to go back. We were trapped!

To add to our concerns, we saw that a car had gone over the cliff, but without a phone to call for help and no place to pull over, it was too dangerous to attempt anything. It was a dangerous situation and Ed's fatigue began to show when the car came very close to the edge a couple times due to lack of markings and impaired visibility.

We had never experienced anything as terrifying as this before. We sang non-stop so our girls would be distracted, and of course we were praying the whole time. It was a very perilous situation.

We had hoped for another driver to overtake us so we could follow behind them but hadn't seen another car except for the one that went over the cliff. We continued singing and praying and then suddenly a white car passed us, and to our relief slowed down and stayed right in front of us. Through the fog and rain, we managed to keep our eyes on its dim taillights. It seemed that the driver knew the area well because he took pains to signal with his arm out the window when to slow down and when we were approaching a curve. All we could see was his bright white shirtsleeve and his hand signaling out the window.

What a relief! We were so thankful to the Lord for having brought this friendly Brazilian, or whoever he was, to guide us. After a while, the white car turned to the right and disappeared. I told Ed, *"Don't lose him. Turn right! Stay with him!"* But when we got to where he left the road, there was nothing there, not even an intersection. We wondered where he had gone, and more pressing still, what were we going to do without his help?

But when we looked ahead, we saw bright lights, a four-lane highway, and no more rain. Within minutes we had arrived in Curitiba. At that moment it dawned on us that the Lord had sent an angel to guide and protect us.

Jehovah-Jireh took care of us. Together with the girls we began singing a victory song that after that became our anthem when traveling on the road:

It is God who has given us the victory
It is God who has given us the victory
It is God who has given us the victory
Hallelujah, Hallelujah,
Hallelujah. Amen.

It is so comforting to know that the Lord dispatches angels to protect us. Not long afterward, we had an opportunity to experience this, but in a far more dramatic manner.

18 ANGELS SENT TO RESCUE US

The angel of the Lord encamps around those who fear Him, and rescues them. (Psalm 34:7)

On another occasion, when traveling from San Nicolas to Buenos Aires, we were miraculously delivered from sure death by angels.

Ed, Evelyn and I were in the lead car, and Marilyn, Jesica and Karina, along with two of their friends (Jonathan and Debbie), rode in the second vehicle. It began to rain heavily and the road became slippery. We came upon a badly designed underpass. It had a pillar separating the fast lane from the other two lanes without any markings or illumination of any kind. In fact, we learned later that it was a spot where accidents happened regularly, especially when the road was flooded, as it was that particular day.

Ed avoided the dangerous pillar, but we both wondered aloud if the second car would be as successful. As our car was coming out of the underpass, we heard a loud noise, like an explosion. We immediately feared for the children in the other car. Ed pulled over to the side of the road and ran in the rain while I followed with Evelyn as fast as I could. When we got to the other side of the underpass, we saw that the second car was embedded into the pillar. Steam was coming out of the engine, it was leaking oil, and the doors were stuck. Ed pulled vigorously until they gave and one by one our kids and their friends came out, bleeding but alive.

There was tremendous confusion and everyone was in shock. Bags and belongings were scattered everywhere, and a band of highway robbers that had been waiting for an accident to happen were closing in for the loot. It was an extremely difficult and dangerous situation, complicated by the fact that in those days there were no cell phones or emergency services, and the police did not patrol the highways at night, especially on rainy days. We didn't know how badly injured our girls and their friends were so we quickly mounted a triage to assess their condition. As long as they were alive, we didn't care if the robbers took everything else.

The crowd (a mixture of curious folks and criminals) was growing and closing in when, all of a sudden, we heard a booming and commanding voice, "Everybody freeze and back off right now!" That stranger took control of the crowd, informed us that he was taking us to a nearby hospital in his vehicle, and told Ed to follow him.

I was amazed at what was happening. Once we were inside his car, I asked, "Sir, who are you?" He simply said, "I was sent to help. Everything is under control." And he definitely had everything under control because when we got to the hospital he gave swift orders to the personnel until everybody was placed in medical bays.

> He simply said, "I was sent to help. Everything is under control."

After I made the rounds, checking that no one was fatally injured, I went looking for him to express my gratitude but he was nowhere to be found. I went to the admissions desk and asked the lady in charge where the man that had come with us was. She gave me a puzzled look and said, "Madam, no one came with you. You came by yourself with the kids."

I insisted that a man had brought us in his vehicle and had given orders to the emergency personnel. Again, she said, "No, there was no one else with you." I went to the parking lot to look for his vehicle but there was nothing there either. At that moment I remembered his words in the car, "I was sent to help," and it dawned on me that he was an angel sent by God.

When I reconnected with Ed after both of us had made the rounds one more time and were comparing notes on who was where and what their condition was, to our dismay we discovered that we were missing Debbie. After checking one more time, with hearts pounding, we realized that we had forgotten her at the accident site.

Ed took off in his car like a rocket, praying all the way. We had already concluded that the luggage and our belongings would be gone, as well as any removable car parts because that is how highway pirates operate, but losing a beautiful American teenager girl would be an irreparable tragedy.

When Ed got to the accident site, he found our luggage neatly arranged in a pile on the side of the road, and the car with nothing missing. He also saw a van parked at the curve and Marilyn's friend seated inside, safe and sound next to a friendly-looking man. Ed led Debbie to his car, and with the help of the stranger, loaded our belongings which he had been watching over in our absence.

Ed asked him, "Sir, how can I reward you for what you have done for us?" To this, he replied very matter of factly, with words similar to the ones I had heard earlier, "I was sent to help. No reward is necessary," then turned around and walked away.

As Ed drove away, he couldn't see him in the rearview mirror. He and his car were gone as mysteriously as they had appeared following the accident. Ed asked Marilyn's friend if she knew his name or who he was. She replied, "I saw him before at several of the church meetings." But Ed did not recall having seen him before.

Who was this person? Undoubtedly, he was another angel, just like the first one who rescued us from the robbers when they were closing in right after the crash.

We later discovered more details that confirmed divine intervention. In front of the column was a rounded man-made "boulder" that served to protect the column from crashes like the one we experienced. The car (a sturdy Ford Falcon with the bench style front seat) hit the "boulder" head-on and squarely, as though it was guided. The crash shrunk the car by a full three feet. The shape of the "boulder," however, lifted the engine upward, keeping it from entering the interior of the car. The impact popped the windshield out and it struck Jonathan in the front seat just above his right eye. But what could easily have been a serious or deadly head injury only scathed him. Karina was sitting in the middle of the front seat and just prior to the crash had folded her legs under her on the seat. That saved her feet from being severely injured or severed by the portable air conditioning unit that became detached by force of the impact. Only God could have orchestrated all those "coincidental" details.

The next day, Omar Cabrera Sr., a dear friend of ours, came all the way from his hometown—about 500 miles away—to pray for us and to let us know that a couple hours before the accident happened, the Holy Spirit warned him that friends of his were the target of a demonic attack to kill them. Immediately he and his wife Marfa went into their prayer room where Ed found him when he called past midnight to let them know what had taken place. It

> He and his car were gone as mysteriously as they had appeared.

was true that the devil was actively targeting us, but the Lord was making provision not only to deliver us, but also to teach us that angels are real and that their protection is essential to carry out our ministry. Like the story in Acts chapter 12, the prayers of the church and angelic intervention delivered God's servants from death.

Do a search in your Bible for the word angels. You will be blessed to see how common it was for them to be dispatched to protect and deliver God's children.

19 ANGELS ON ASSIGNMENT

Years later, when we had moved to San Jose where we established our new ministry headquarters, we were blessed again by an angelic intervention. Our daughter Evelyn was beginning to drive and I was a bit worried, as I'm sure many mothers are, because of the new dangers our youngsters become exposed to behind the wheel. Every time she left the house I would wait for her, praying off and on until she got back, especially at night since back then we didn't have cell phones.

I asked the Lord to give me peace and He did it in a rather unusual way. A few weeks after Evelyn got her driver's license, we went to see a play that was about an innocent looking girl driving her car, unaware of all the angels that were providing protection for her safety as she sang "Angels Watching Over Me."

After I saw that play, the fear left me because the Lord used it to remind me that angels are assigned to protect us, especially His children. When Evelyn came home that night, she told us an amazing story of what happened to her on the way. She was about to cross an intersection with a four-way stop (traffic in every direction must make a full stop before proceeding in the order in which they arrived). It was her turn to go next when her car stalled. At that precise moment, another car came barreling through the intersection she was about to cross at extremely high speed, completely disregarding the stop sign.

As she watched in shock while the car zoomed by, it dawned on her that she could have been in a serious, perhaps deadly, collision if her car had not stalled. As she was pondering this, she saw an angel sitting on the hood of her car and

EVELYN WITH HER CAR

immediately realized that she had been spared by its intervention. It must have been a "mechanically savvy angel" because he knew how to disable the engine until danger had passed!

Take heart that angels are watching over you and your loved ones when their life or welfare is in danger. When Peter was in prison expecting to be executed the next day, an angel came into his cell and set him free (see Acts 12:7). When the ship Paul was sailing on as a prisoner was about to succumb to a violent storm, an angel reassured him that he and everyone else on the ship would not perish (Acts 27:23-24). In both cases, the situation looked humanly hopeless until angels dispatched by God turned chaos into order and despair into hope.

Angels are watching over you and your loved ones right now. Thank God for that extra protection.

EVELYN IS GLAD THAT ANGELS PROTECT YOUNG DRIVERS BECAUSE HER SON MAXI LOVES DRIVING!

20 THE GUN BARREL, JESUS AND ME

We continued to experience dangerous times in Rosario. My brother's crusade was a success, in spite of the turmoil rocking the country and the dangers we continued to be exposed to daily, especially Ed who traveled all over organizing the follow-up to the crusade to make sure the new believers were incorporated into local churches.

Evelyn was one-week-old and I was not feeling well, so I went to the pharmacy down the street to buy a decongestant. As I was waiting to pay for it, two very mean-looking (and armed) robbers came into the store. They tied up the owners with the telephone wires they ripped off the wall, then ordered all of us customers to lie down on the floor and demanded that the pharmacist give them a specific drug (a narcotic) they were after. When he told them he'd run out of it, they became agitated and quickly cleaned out the cash register.

I knew they would try to get money and jewelry from those of us on the floor, so while they were looking the other way I took off my wedding ring and hid it under my blouse. While the ring—that meant so much to me—was safe now, my greatest worry was for our new baby at home. What if they killed me? She and her sisters would be orphans. Who would take care of them? And what about Ed, who loved me so much? I began praying quietly but fervently for protection. I knew the robbers' threats to kill us were real because a week earlier there had been a similar armed robbery at a pharmacy nearby with multiple fatalities.

After taking as much money and jewelry as they could from us, one of the men pointed his gun at me and demanded more. It was a dangerous moment and the outcome could have been fatal. Emboldened by the Lord, I told him, "In the name of Jesus, you are not going to kill us."

He immediately began to shake, and with a panicked look on his face shouted to his accomplice, "Let's get out of here!"

We were safe! I ran all the way home and straight into Ed's arms where together we thanked the Lord for His protection. Rather than being intimidated by the dangers, we continued to serve Him. This verse became a source of continuous strength: "The name of the Lord is a strong tower; the righteous runs into it and is safe" (Proverbs 18:10).

21 THE CHAPEL: THE POINT OF INCEPTION

After Rosario, Ed organized crusades for Luis in five cities in Uruguay, touching the entire nation. We were excited and looking forward to the entire Southern Cone opening up when once again dreadful news hit us. Ed developed symptoms of what the doctors suspected to be a life-threatening disease. It was shocking because we had worked so diligently for revival to come to the Southern Cone and we were beginning to see encouraging signs, especially growing unity among pastors.

With Ed's health deteriorating rapidly, we went back to the U.S. with our four daughters where he was diagnosed with an incurable auto-immune disease and given two years to live. The doctors told him, "We don't think we can help you much, but you can help us study this disease," which was medical lingo for, "We would like you to become a guinea pig."

Ed agreed and had to go twice a week to San Francisco for an experimental treatment that included *plasmaphoresis*, a risky procedure because it removed all the antibodies in his blood, leaving only red and white cells, and replaced the lost fluids with plasma. The absence of antibodies meant that for a few days after each treatment, a minor infection could turn fatal very quickly. He also received 16 intramuscular injections daily, chemotherapy every other week, and massive doses of cortisone and other drugs. All of this was just to keep him alive, not to cure him since there was no known cure. We knew that money couldn't buy it because Aristotle Onassis—Jacqueline Kennedy's second husband—had died of the same disease, and he had money to burn.

Ed was used to doing the work of five men so it wasn't easy for him to be sidelined. After much prayer, we resigned from the Luis Palau Team which wasn't easy because we loved Luis and the team, but the clock was ticking and every day that went by meant one less day remaining in the two-year prognosis. It

> All of this was just to keep him alive, not to cure him.

was shortly after our resignation from the Palau Team that the Lord gave us a burden for the 109 towns within a 100-mile radius of our property in San Nicolas. Ed said, "According to the doctors, I won't be around to evangelize those places, so let's build a prayer chapel where others can intercede, and God will surely call someone else to go."

During the treatment in the U.S. (where we had relocated permanently due to his medical condition), whenever Ed's symptoms subsided enough, he would get on a plane and go to Argentina to oversee the building of the chapel at our emerging retreat center. He would return to the U.S. for treatment when he'd reached his limit physically, and once he'd recovered enough strength, he would go back. This went on for months; he never stopped because it was a race against time. He was always thinking of others and never complained, even in the midst of excruciating pain and disabling weakness, so great was his desire to extend God's Kingdom. We were praying for healing and asking everyone we knew for prayer.

> "...let's build a prayer chapel where others can intercede, and God will surely call someone else to go."

One day, while driving on the road to the retreat center, he cried out, "Lord, I'm not afraid of dying, but I want to know if this illness is unto life or unto death. I need to know how to pray, and more importantly, what to prepare for because I have a young family."

At that precise moment, the presence of the Lord filled the car in such a way that it totally overwhelmed him. He barely made it to the retreat center where for the next six hours the Holy Spirit interceded for him and through him with groaning too deep for the human mind to comprehend as described in Romans 8:26. As he was praying in the Spirit, he was directed to specific promises of power and deliverance in the Bible, and by dawn God had assured Ed that his illness was an illness unto life.

The next morning, when he shared this with a prayer partner who had spent the night in the city, he told Ed that he had received exactly the same message! From that day on, we started to thank God for the healing that was coming instead of asking for it.

Ed's condition did not improve right away; in fact, he was rushed to the Emergency Room twice, but on both occasions, Ed asked people not to pray for healing since he knew it was coming, but rather to join him in thanking God for the healing that would come as per God's word to him. This allowed us to acknowledge the present reality—Ed was very sick—while hanging on to the hope that what God had promised would come to pass.

Eventually Ed was healed, although it was a process and not instantaneous. In the midst of all this, we gave birth to Harvest Evangelism (now Transform Our World). We launched radio and television programs, as well as a Christian newspaper in Argentina to let different denominations learn what was happening in the church at large. We completed construction of the retreat center and were blessed to see people being trained at this property that had once been our weekend home and now was impacting lives. Among those who came to help was an American couple who proposed to build a prayer chapel in memory of a beloved daughter who had passed away on the eve of

> Never could they have imagined the catalytic role that chapel would play in launching a worldwide transformation ministry!

her wedding. Rather than being overwhelmed by that sad memory, they decided to turn it into a blessing. Neither the Canadians who provided the funds to buy the land, nor this couple, could have imagined the catalytic role that chapel would play in evangelizing those towns and eventually in launching a world-wide transformation ministry!

We became aware that the powers of darkness were deeply entrenched in that region when we learned that the worst of those towns was under the spell of a warlock who had 12 disciples, and many famous people (including influential politicians) would go to him to "get healed."

That is why we turned the chapel into a vortex for intercession for the entire region. In the process, we discovered Prayer Evangelism as the most effective way to equip the saints for them to do the work of evangelism. Today, all those towns have a Christian witness, the house where the warlock had his headquarters is now a church, and one of his disciples is its leader.

We learned many lessons through this long trial, especially about intercession and spiritual warfare. We learned how to submit to God in order to be able to resist the devil for him to flee according to James 4:4, instead of *ignoring* him and *hoping* that he would flee. These lessons became so important when the Lord led us to Resistencia and other cities immersed in witchcraft. But above everything else, we learned that the mess we may be experiencing today would become our *message* tomorrow if we surrender ourselves to Him. Amazing how much God can do when we give Him what we have, even if it is a rapidly deteriorating body! Small beginnings in God's hands are just that, a beginning that is bound to grow like the light of dawn described in Proverbs 4:18. Trust Him because God is always faithful!

Chapel
TRAINING CENTER
San Nicolás, Argentina

22 RESISTENCIA: THE LAUNCHING PAD

The dramatic experiences involving the Chapel prepared us for the location that would become the international launching pad for our ministry: Resistencia.

The Lord led us to this city in northern Argentina to test the groundbreaking principles that later would be the subject of Ed's first two best-selling books, *That None Should Perish* and *Prayer Evangelism*, on a larger scale. A successful prototype was developed there that eventually was emulated all over the world, but not without first facing brutal spiritual warfare.

Resistencia was under the evil spell of what Paul describes in Ephesians 6:12 as *governors of the darkness*, two of which were familiar to the population in the city. One was called "San La Muerte" (Saint Death) and falsely promised those that worshipped him a painless death; the other was "Curupi," the ruler of love and lust. They were the source of the grim spiritual climate in the region. No wonder Resistencia was known as a cemetery for evangelism.

Dave and Sue Thompson had joined our team by then, and courageously decided to move there with their kids to encourage and envision the pastors to believe that the entire city could be reached for Christ and, as a result, those principalities dethroned.

The challenge was huge because out of 400,000 inhabitants, only 5,143 were known to be believers. To compound the situation, they attended 70 churches of which 68 were the result of a division. At first, only seven pastors out of seventy agreed to get together to pray weekly, but God used them to start a chain reaction that in two years, through

prayer evangelism, doubled the membership of the churches in the city. That growth has continued, making it the region with the largest Christian population in the nation.

> ...young people who went to help in Resistencia remember how those days changed their lives...

Many of the young people who went to help in Resistencia remember how those days changed their lives, and today they are in ministry. Chip Ingram, who has developed a very influential ministry and pastors Venture Church in Los Gatos, California, just a couple miles from our offices, is one of them. Chip went there as part of a Christian basketball team that presented the Gospel during halftime, usually by passing out tracts and sharing short testimonies. His life was set on the path that led to him becoming one of the most sought-after speakers in America when Ed asked him to preach during that trip. Chip informed Ed that he couldn't do it because he had never preached before.

Ed asked him, "Have you had your devotions today?"

Chip nodded, "Yes."

Ed inquired, "What passage of Scripture did you read?"

When Chip identified it, Ed said to him, "I'm sure you got some spiritual truths out of it, so that is your message for tonight. Go preach it!" He handed him the microphone and Chip's life was never the same.

In addition to countless people that have been touched by our ministry, there are cities all over the world being transformed by the scriptural principles that came to light in Argentina—during a time when we were still in the midst of a very dark canyon with Ed fighting for survival, me facing the real possibility of widowhood (a frightening throwback to my childhood memories), and our daughters potentially left orphans. But God is more than faithful; He is extravagantly faithful, full of mercy and compassion. Ed and I know without a doubt that every good thing in our ministry is a trophy of His grace, often built by Him using broken pieces (like us), and for that we give God all the honor and glory.

Today, by God's grace, we have the immense privilege of leading a network of influencers from around the globe that is dedicated to seeing the will of God done on earth, just as it is in heaven. We love to see people come to Christ and have a passion to see them grow and take the power and presence of God to their spheres of influence to change the world. Ed is a transformational leader and many refer to him as the "father of transformation," but he remains humble. Even though he is a best-selling author and the producer of over 45 documentaries, he doesn't boast about it but instead gives all the glory to God.

Through the years we've been involved in many major catalytic events. In 1997, Ed was part of the platform team during the Stand in the Gap "Million Man" gathering in Washington, D.C., organized by Promise Keepers. It was an amazing event, with men on their faces before God, renewing their commitment to the Lord and to their families, and millions tuning in to the live broadcast.

In 1998, we hosted "Light the Nation," a nationwide outreach held at Madison Square Garden in New York. It was a ground-breaking event broadcast to 547 cities all over America to teach believers how to change the spiritual climate in their communities.

In 2008, Ed spoke from a packed stadium in Cape Town to the entire continent of Africa (58 countries) via a combination of radio and TV, invited by his friend Graham Power who organized the event.

Most recently, in early 2020, Ed was one of the speakers at *The Send*, a mega event in Sao Paulo, Brazil. Held in three stadiums simultaneously, the speakers were transferred between venues and 150,000 people attended in person while hundreds of thousands watched the live stream!

In addition to addressing large crowds, he loves counseling and mentoring people one on one. As we travel around the world, we come across many who tell us how much the ministry has blessed them. Here are five of the hundreds of letters we've received:

You are one of the brightest and greatest strategic thinkers and planners in our generation. I am so proud to know you and walk with you. You will have the greatest impact in the coming year that you have known. The Lord will use you in rallying the troops as never before! God Bless You!

—James Goll

One of the things I appreciate most about you is the way you teach how to love and be a blessing to your family. You have been an example in that and the Lord has honored you with four wonderful daughters who have followed the Lord and are a blessing to all those around you. The Lord also gave you a beautiful, loving wife. Bill and I enjoyed working with you and your team for the way you all love the Lord. May our Father keep on blessing you and your dear ones during the coming years.

—Annie Kennedy (Served the Lord with us for years in Argentina with her husband Bill)

Ed Silvoso is one of the clearest, most coherent, thoroughly biblical thinkers we have today.

—Jack Hayford (Chancellor Emeritus, The King's University)

Your evangelism, prayers and teaching have changed many lives, including my own.

—Cindy Nardi (Teacher at Valley Christian School where Ed is Chaplain to the Board)

Knowing you has changed my life from the inside out! Not just for the transformation principles you teach, but how you model it on every level of your life. Watching you love and show grace in the most stressful of situations to all people has had a forever impact on me. You are consistently generous to give back financially, relationally, physically with your time and energy and spiritually with your prayers and discernment. The way you father your family, and adopted sons and daughters, is so beautiful to watch. And your drive for life inspires me to be even more passionate for the Kingdom of God alongside you. How could I leave out your love story with Ruth that is unique and declares true love to so many. Thank you for modeling true, pure, deep, honest love and always putting her first.

—Karissa Stafford (served on our team for eight years)

Folks like these are accomplishing great things for God. It's an honor to be connected to them in God's work, but it all goes back to a very small beginning…

23 WHAT WAS WATERED WITH TEARS...

Rosario is a city that is close to our hearts for a number of reasons. It is the birthplace of our two younger daughters, Evelyn and Jesica. It is also where we introduced the Luis Palau Team to the nation through "Plan Rosario."

Ed documented the favorable outcome of "Plan Rosario" in his book *That None Should Perish*, so I won't get into that except to say that it introduced new seeds into new ground, and the next generation of pastors applied the principles with even greater results after we left the city.

Rosario was also the place where Ed got sick, I was robbed at gunpoint, we dodged bullets, and one of our daughters barely escaped being kidnapped. Very few saw the sacrifice it cost us, or the fruit of Plan Rosario, because we did not talk about these painful things and because fruit takes time to show.

After we left the city in 1978 (with Ed sick and not without considerable sadness), a younger generation of leaders began to apply the principles we taught. In fact, Norberto Carlini, who was a young seminary graduate and part of Ed's team, today has one of the most dynamic congregations in the city.

When Ed went back many years later to host a national conference on transformation, Norberto organized a reception to honor him for having watered with tears the seeds that had produced the harvest they were enjoying. He said this on national television:

> "Ed left everything here in Argentina and we did not appreciate it because we did not understand it. So, others, in the strangest places overseas, took the seed to their countries and got great results. And we are still looking at the seed he left and wondering if it will work."

Then he addressed Ed (who was in the audience) directly:

> "Ed, forgive us, and please do not abandon us. We want to hook up like a caboose to this train that is going around the entire world. Let's keep on running, and I believe that from here in Argentina we are opening a new chapter, and great testimonies are going to flow from this place."

Another pastor, who now leads a mega church and a powerful television ministry, put it this way:

> "Carlini and I, along with others who were in our teens or early twenties back then, watched closely how you worked and how the older folks mistreated you. And we decided that when we grew up we wanted to be like you and not like them."

Such is the generation that is leading the Church in Rosario, most of whom were young kids when we first went, but today are men and women of God. One of those pastors is Aldo Martin and his wife Roxi, and this is their story.

One Sunday in 2012, a member of our congregation approached me with this prayer request: "Pastor, my 15-year-old son has been kidnapped. Can you help me get him back?"

"What do you mean by kidnapped? In our city there are no kidnappings," was my answer. She insisted, "Pastor, it's true; my son was kidnapped by the drug cartel and is being held prisoner in a 'bunker.'"

"What is a bunker?" I asked.

The woman, now growing impatient as a result of my ignorance of what was going on in the city, explained to me that a bunker is a small hermetically sealed room from where drugs are sold, and that her son had been kidnapped to do that since, as a minor, charges could not be brought against him.

ALDO & ROXI MARTIN

I then asked a third and totally naïve question: "Why didn't you report it to the police?"

This lady had already lost what little patience she had left and answered me with obvious frustration, "But pastor, the police are involved. They are in cahoots with the cartel! Please pray. I want my son back!"

I prayed with very little faith. It was the first time I was made aware of the seriousness of what was happening in my beloved city. In the Seminary where I studied, there were no classes on "How to rescue kidnapped kids from a drug bunker." I was at a total loss as to what to do next. Nevertheless, we began to pray in our congregation, crying out to the Lord since we didn't know what to do.

...the next generation of pastors applied the principles with even greater results after we left the city.

One of the church members, Gregorio, lived in Barrio Las Flores, which at the time was the center of drug trafficking in the region. Brokenhearted over the violence destroying his neighborhood, he began to pray on site and one day God spoke to him: "Gregorio, who do I have in your neighborhood that will glorify me?" He fell on his knees, raised his hands to heaven, and responded to the Lord with a resounding, "Here I am, Lord. Send me!"

His neighborhood was the worst in the city: extreme poverty, abandonment, violence, death, drug trafficking, robberies. The police had lost control and darkness ruled. There was no public bus or taxi service available because drivers were being robbed and killed; even ambulances were held at gunpoint and valuables stolen! But on that particular day at Gregorio's house, a light went on in his heart. A few days later, elections were held to elect the president of the Barrio. And who do you think entered himself as a candidate? Gregorio! And he won by four votes!

The following Sunday he came to church and proudly announced: "Pastor, they elected me president of Barrio Las Flores."

It took me totally by surprise, and in my mind, I thought, What a mess you've gotten yourself into! But while I was preaching, God spoke to me and said, "Anoint him as the pastor of that Barrio."

I stopped the message, called Gregorio forward, and anointed him as "pastor" of his neighborhood as Ed Silvoso had taught us in person and through his books, particularly Anointed for Business. The following week, Gregorio showed me a photo of his "office," the closest thing to the Gates of Hades you could imagine! The families in the neighborhood were so poor that every time one of their own (usually a minor) was murdered, they borrowed that office (that doubled as a community center) to conduct the funeral service. The smell of death and grief was all over the place.

Around this time, it "just so happened" that Michael Brown and Tony Mitchell from Vallejo, a city in the San Francisco Bay Area that was impacted by Ed and Ruth Silvoso's ministry, were in Argentina, equipping regional leaders in transformation. When they heard about Gregorio's new position in the barrio, they asked him, "How can we help?"

Gregorio suggested that they provide supplies to paint the run-down community center, so the Ekklesia in Vallejo (through Michael and Tony who were in town) provided the resources. Then, with every stroke of the paintbrush, a blessing was deposited on what until then had been the embodiment of the Gates of Hades. Soon Gregorio was emboldened to ask God to send people with barrio-sized solutions. The divine sign would be that they would ask, "How can I help you, Gregorio?"

First came the mayor of Rosario, then the governor of the province, and finally the national minister of security, all posing the same question: "What can I do for you?"

The latter deployed troops to demolish the drug bunkers. The other two brought restoration and renovation. Today, Barrio Las Flores has freshly paved streets, a sewer system, streetlights and a new school. The new regional hospital (the largest in the province) is being built there, as well as a brand-new train station. That Jesus had come to the neighborhood was never more in evidence than when, for the first time ever, over ten thousand people in Barrio Las Flores felt safe enough to leave their homes to publicly gather for the proclamation of the Gospel by renowned Argentine evangelist Carlos Annacondia, with thousands making decisions for Christ. That Kingdom authority is now moving beyond the boundaries of the barrio as the growing Ekklesia of Rosario regularly ministers to both the mayor and the governor.

I was not a pastor when Ed and Ruth first came to Rosario, but the transformation seeds they planted and watered with their tears are bearing much fruit and fruit that keeps expanding.

Rosario is situated in the Province of Santa Fe and has been governed by socialists who take pride in their agnosticism or atheism and in advocating a humanistic social agenda. As such, they are the least likely to be open to spiritual things, much less to the Church. Nevertheless, Aldo and Roxi Martin adopted the governor spiritually and began to practice prayer evangelism, blessing him in their prayers and fellowshipping with him "a la Luke 10." They were also able to minister to the felt needs of his family, leading him to experience goodness, peace and joy—in essence, the Kingdom of God.

As a result, the socialist government led by the governor convened a meeting with pastors at Aldo's place and asked them to consider mentoring fifty thousand youngsters who had gotten in trouble with the law. These are teenagers who neither work nor study and many of them have already done time in juvenile hall or prison. In essence, they are a social time bomb.

The government specifically asked that every participating church turn its building into a training center three days a week where those kids could learn life and work skills. The government offered to pay for the construction of workshops—carpentry, plumbing, computer labs, etc.—on church property, and would provide financial support for the students and full salary for two church leaders to serve as mentors for every 50 youth. As if this were not already a supremely extraordinary development, this socialist government also asked that 33 percent of the training time be devoted to Bible classes. Basically, the government asked the Ekklesia to disciple the province. This offer is indeed an extraordinary miracle! Its full potential is still to be played out but the fact it was made speaks eloquently about the power of the Gospel when it's taken to the public arena, something that was at the heart of "Plan Rosario," albeit embryonically back then.

> Basically, the government asked the Ekklesia to disciple the province.

It goes without saying how much joy this story brings to us. It shows that God is debtor to no one, that when we preach the Word of God and serve Him in spite of the trials that come our way, the Word always bears fruit, even if it takes time.

The stories in the next section, "From the World," testify to this. What began in a small chapel in Argentina has now gone all over the world. God is faithful!

PART 2

FROM THE PAST
TO THE PRESENT
AND INTO
THE FUTURE...

Before moving to stories from around the world, I chose to share those from our immediate family—our children and grandchildren – because as the old missionary adage states, "The light that shines the farthest is the one that shines the brightest at its base," in this case, the home.

The following stories testify to that. But first, allow me to introduce my family in this family portrait, and then read on and be edified!

24 LOVE STORY BY THE HOLY SPIRIT HIMSELF

The Holy Spirit, who inspired the Scriptures, left us the best love stories in the Bible. I want to highlight one of them—used by "divine permission," of course—that shows how God makes provision for the right spouse, one "made by God" for His children. This is a key point because finding the right spouse is the foundation for a happy home. Read, rejoice and apply it:

Now Abraham was old, advanced in age; and the Lord had blessed Abraham in every way. Abraham said to his servant, the oldest of his household, who had charge of all that he owned, "Please place your hand under my thigh, and I will make you swear by the Lord, the God of heaven and the God of earth, that you shall not take a wife for my son from the daughters of the Canaanites, among whom I live, but you will go to my country and to my relatives, and take a wife for my son Isaac." The Lord, the God of heaven will send His angel before you, and you will take a wife for my son from there. But if the woman is not willing to follow you, then you will be free from this my oath; only do not take my son back there." So the servant swore to him concerning this matter.

Then the servant took ten camels from the camels of his master, and set out with a variety of good things of his master's in his hand; and he arose and went to the city of Nahor. He made the camels kneel down outside the city by the well of water at evening time, the time when women go out to draw water. He said, "O Lord, the God of my master Abraham, please grant me success today, and show loving kindness to my master Abraham. Behold, I am standing by the spring, and the daughters of the men of the city are coming out to draw water; now may it be that the girl to whom I say, 'Please let down your jar so that I may drink,' and who answers, 'Drink, and I will water your camels also'—may she be the one whom You have appointed for Your servant Isaac; and by this I will know that You have shown lovingkindness to my master."

Before he had finished speaking, behold, Rebekah who was born to Bethuel the son of Milcah, the wife of Abraham's brother Nahor, came out with her jar on her shoulder. The girl was very beautiful, a virgin, and no man had had relations with her; and she went down to the spring and filled her jar and came up. Then the servant ran to meet her, and said, "Please let me drink a little water from your jar." She said, "Drink, my lord"; and she quickly lowered her jar to her hand, and gave him a drink. Now when she had finished giving him a drink, she said, "I will draw also for your camels until they have finished drinking." So she quickly emptied her jar into the trough, and ran back to the well to draw, and she drew for all his camels. Meanwhile, the man was gazing at her in silence, to know whether the Lord had made his journey successful or not.

When the camels had finished drinking, the man took a gold ring weighing a half-shekel and two bracelets for her wrists weighing ten shekels in gold, and said, "Whose daughter are you? Please tell me, is there room for us to lodge in your father's house?" She said to him, "I am the daughter of Bethuel, the son of Milcah, whom she bore to Nahor." Again she said to him, "We have plenty of both straw and feed, and room to lodge in." Then the man bowed low and worshiped the Lord. He said, "Blessed be the Lord, the God of my master Abraham, who has not forsaken His loving-kindness and His truth toward my master; as for me, the Lord has guided me in the way to the house of my master's brothers."

Then the girl ran and told her mother's household about these things. Now Rebekah had a brother whose name was Laban; and Laban ran outside to the man at the spring. When he saw the ring and the bracelets on his sister's wrists, and when he heard the words of Rebekah his sister, saying, "This is what the man said to me," he went to the man; and behold, he was standing by the camels at the spring. And he said, "Come in, blessed of the Lord! Why do you stand outside since I have prepared the house, and a place for the camels?" So the man entered the house. Then Laban unloaded the camels, and he gave straw and feed to the camels, and water to wash his feet and the feet of the men who were with him. But when food was set before him to eat, he said, "I will not eat until I have told my business." And he said, "Speak on." So he said, "I am Abraham's servant. The Lord has greatly blessed my master, so that he has become rich; and He has given him flocks and herds, and silver and gold, and servants and maids, and camels and donkeys. Now Sarah my master's wife bore a son to my master in her old age, and he has given him all that he has. My master made me swear, saying, 'You shall not take a wife for my son from the daughters of the Canaanites, in whose land I live; but you shall go to my father's house and to my relatives, and take a wife for my son.

"So I came today to the spring, and said, 'O Lord, the God of my master Abraham, if now You will make my journey on which I go successful; behold, I am standing by the spring, and may it be that the maiden who comes out to draw, and to whom I say, "Please let me drink a little water from your jar"; and she will say to me, "You drink, and I will draw for your camels also"; let her be the woman whom the Lord has appointed for my master's son.'

"Before I had finished speaking in my heart, behold, Rebekah came out with her jar on her shoulder, and went down to the spring and drew, and I said to her, 'Please let me drink.' She quickly lowered her jar from her shoulder, and said, 'Drink, and I will water your camels also'; so I drank, and she watered the camels also. Then I asked her, and said, 'Whose daughter are you?' And she said, 'The daughter of Bethuel, Nahor's son, whom Milcah bore to him'; and I put the ring on her nose, and the bracelets on her wrists. And I bowed low and worshiped the Lord, and blessed the Lord, the God of my master Abraham, who had guided me in the right way to take the daughter of my master's kinsman for his son. So now if you are going to deal kindly and truly with my master, tell me; and if not, let me know, that I may turn to the right hand or the left."

Then Laban and Bethuel replied, "The matter comes from the Lord; so we cannot speak to you bad or good. Here is Rebekah before you, take her and go, and let her be the wife of your master's son, as the Lord has spoken."

When Abraham's servant heard their words, he bowed himself to the ground before the Lord. The servant brought out articles of silver and articles of gold, and garments, and gave them to Rebekah; he also gave precious things to her brother and to her mother. Then he and the men who were with him ate and drank and spent the night. When they arose in the morning, he said, "Send me away to my master." But her brother and her mother said, "Let the girl stay with us a few days, say ten; afterward she may go." He said to them, "Do not delay me, since the Lord has prospered my way. Send me away that I may go to my master." And they said, "We will call the girl and consult her wishes." Then they called Rebekah and said to her, "Will you go with this man?" And she said, "I will go." Thus they sent away their sister Rebekah and her nurse with Abraham's servant and his men.

They blessed Rebekah and said to her,

"May you, our sister,

Become thousands of ten thousands,

And may your descendants possess

The gate of those who hate them."

Then Rebekah arose with her maids, and they mounted the camels and followed the man. So the servant took Rebekah and departed.

Now Isaac had come from going to Beer-lahai-roi; for he was living in the Negev. Isaac went out to meditate in the field toward evening; and he lifted up his eyes and looked, and behold, camels were coming. Rebekah lifted up her eyes, and when she saw Isaac she dismounted from the camel. She said to the servant, "Who is that man walking in the field to meet us?" And the servant said, "He is my master." Then she took her veil and covered herself. The servant told Isaac all the things that he had done. Then Isaac brought her into his mother Sarah's tent, and he took Rebekah, and she became his wife, and he loved her; thus Isaac was comforted after his mother's death.

It's inspiring to read how the Lord led Abraham and his servant Eliezer to find the wife He had prepared for his son Isaac. Ed and I know that this can happen today because the Holy Spirit led us in a similar way to find each other. We taught our girls to trust God to guide them to the right husband, and He did!

They are all happily married and have blessed us with wonderful grandchildren who are also trusting the Holy Spirit to lead them to the right spouse.

THE HOLY SPIRIT LED EVELYN TO KARL,
HER GOD-MADE HUSBAND.

25 CHILDREN ARE AN AWESOME GIFT FROM GOD

I enjoy reflecting back on the day when each one of our precious daughters was born. They are married now to wonderful men of God and have given us grandchildren who love the Lord and are filled with the Holy Spirit.

Our first daughter, Karina, was born in San Nicolas. The same doctor that 23 years earlier delivered Ed, delivered her. The board gave us a private room at the hospital since Ed was the CEO, and a cook was assigned to serve us whatever we wanted to eat. We took advantage of such treatment and stayed several days beyond what a normal delivery requires. Friends and business associates sent so many flowers that our room looked like a flower shop. We also received beautiful gifts, including a British baby carriage, a gold ring and earrings (customary in Argentina), and toys and stuffed animals of all sizes for Karina.

KARINA

What a joy it was to have the blessing of our new, healthy and beautiful baby girl, Karina Andrea. We were so happy and thankful to the Lord for this gift. Today, she is serving the Lord as the Executive Administrative Assistant to Dr. Clifford Daugherty, the President of Valley Christians Schools, a school that is transforming public education in the San Francisco Bay Area, and she and her husband Gary own a transformation company.

I became pregnant with our second daughter, Marilyn, when we were studying in Portland, Oregon. Living away from Argentina made that pregnancy very special. Everything was new and different in a nice way. But the baby was overdue, which was getting a bit concerning, so at the first signs of a contraction we were ready to go to the hospital. We had heard that you could run the red lights if you were on the way to the hospital to have a baby, and that the police would even escort you…but we didn't run into any policemen and made it in time without running any red lights!

This precious nine-pound, six-ounce baby was born on a snowy January 20th. What a blessing, what a miracle! I looked out the win-

MARILYN

dow that day and saw the beautiful American flag that I like so much. One advantage of having such a big baby was that she was strong and slept through the night from day one! We joked that the rain was the reason she turned out to be so big because it rained so much in Portland. Today, she is six feet tall. Praise God for the gift of life. What a joy, a beautiful life. Marilyn oversees the finances and accounting services in our ministry, and her husband Ken is our Development Director. They mentor young adults on how to be an Ekklesia in the marketplace in Silcon Valley where they live. Thank you, Jesus, for sweet Marilyn Ruth.

Our third daughter, Evelyn, was born in Rosario after we re-turned to Argentina to organize my brother Luis's crusade there. She was born at the British Hospital the last weekend of the crusade and we were able to take her to the stadium for the closing service. Luis introduced her to the crowd and thou-sands of people welcomed and blessed her. She was peacefully in my arms next to the platform with beautiful rosy cheeks as cameras clicked and flashes went off. From that day on, believ-ers in Rosario called her "the crusade baby." What a joy and a great blessing the Lord entrusted to us. Today, she is the Chief Operations Officer at Transform Our World and also leads a coalition of transformation women. She and her husband Karl own a transformational professional apparel business. Precious Evelyn Marisel.

EVELYN

JESICA

Our fourth daughter, Jesica, was also born in Rosario, at the Parque Hospital across from a beautiful park. I felt such a connection when I finally laid eyes on her after carrying her inside me for nine months. The nurse placed her on my chest and I could feel her heart beating so fast, and when Ed pressed the tip of his finger into her tiny hand, she wrapped hers around it. Jesica was welcoming us as much as we were welcoming her. Jesica Jacqueline was a healthy, beautiful baby, and she is such a blessing and joy to our family!

I nursed Jesica, as well as the other three girls, for as long as I could. While we were in the hospital, whenever the nurses came to take them back to the nursery, I would make sure I was nursing them so I could keep them longer, and when we told them we wanted to keep them in our room all night, they allowed it. This is very common nowadays but it wasn't back then. Today, Jesica and her husband Benjy lead the Transformation Family Track in our ministry and have turned their home into an Ekklesia that pastors the neighborhood, in addition to ministering to young people and families all over the world.

All four of our daughters are a tremendous blessing and joy. We constantly thank God for their lives, so full of the Holy Spirit.

26 THE POWER OF TEACHING GOD'S WORD TO OUR CHILDREN

It never ceases to amaze me how sensitive children are in spiritual matters. I believe that is the reason why Jesus admonished us to be like children, not with regard to any temporary ignorance or immaturity that will be corrected as they grow, but in relation to the purity of the lenses through which they see life. They are so innocent, so positive, so optimistic, until later on when the evil one, who according to Jesus came to kill, steal and destroy, tries to ruin that. But that can be prevented. Like Nelson Mandela wrote in his memoir, *"No child is born hating or being a racist."* Obviously, that type of socially despicable behavior is learned later in life. And since that is the case, it can be unlearned, and that is the beauty and the power of the Word of God that shows us how to do it.

The following is a good example of such spiritual sensitivity in young people. While I was working on this manuscript, our granddaughters Mia Grace and Emma Elizabeth highlighted for me a selection of verses from Deuteronomy chapter 6 that instruct us to pass on the truths of God to our children and grandchildren. It expresses God's point of view on the value and the benefits of teaching the younger generation so well that I chose to include it here.

> *v.6 These commandments that I give you today are to be on your hearts.*

> *v.7 Impress them on your children. Talk about them when you sit at home and when you walk along the road, when you lie down and when you get up. Tie them as symbols on your hands and bind them on your foreheads. Write them on the doorframes of your houses and on your gates.*

> *v.24 Do what is right and good in the Lord's sight, so that it may go well with you so that we might always prosper and be kept alive.*

> *v.25 And if we are careful to obey all this law before the Lord our God, as he has commanded us, that will be our righteousness.*

> *(Deuteronomy 6:6,7,24,25 NIV)*

In verse 7, we are commanded to impress God's truths on our children all the time: when we sit down and when we are on the road, when we lie down and when we get up. In other words, we must be persistent and intentional. It shouldn't be a chore but a lifestyle. The modern equivalent of tying God's commands on their hands and binding them on their foreheads would be to give them a Bible App with a version for children or youth, depending on their age. Also, play passages of the scriptures on the car audio system while driving them. The Word of God is living and as such it penetrates the mind and the heart, even if listened to passively.

The instruction to write them on the doorposts of the house and gates can be replicated nowadays by hanging pictures of Bible verses on the walls of our home. In our childhood home, my mom displayed two verses. The first one spoke primarily to us, the children, by giving us a spiritual destination with a roadmap to get there, "The path of the righteous is like the light of dawn, that shines brighter and brighter until the full day" (Proverbs 4:18). The second one was the verse that sustained her during difficult times, "We know that God causes all things to work together for good to those who love God" (Romans 8:28).

Making sure that the Word of God is readily available to our children is the best we can do for them to live a victorious life:

"How can a young man keep his way pure? By keeping it according to your word. With all my heart I have sought you; do not let me wander from your commandments. Your word I have treasured in my heart, that I may not sin against you." (Psalm 119:9-11)

MARILYN, EMMA, SERENA, MIA, AND KEN

27 A LEGACY OF FAITH AND ITS IMPACT ON GENERATIONS

Paul reminded Timothy, one of his disciples whom he considered a spiritual son, that he was blessed to be the recipient of faith that upstreamed to his grandmother Lois and his mother Eunice (2 Timothy 1:5). I am sure those two ladies were beaming with pride every time they heard how God was using Timothy.

SERENA

I can relate to that as I see how the faith Ed and I inherited from our own parents has been passed on to our daughters, and through them to each one of our grandchildren. Our daughter Marilyn and her husband Ken are parents to three wonderful girls: Serena, Mia and Emma. Each one of them is a wonderful vessel that God uses every day. This is true of all our daughters and sons-in-law. As an example of that, I share this tribute that Serena presented at the 2017 Global Transformation Conference before delegates from all over the world. Read and be edified!

I want to share about family legacies, specifically my great-grandmother, Abuela Teresa Silvoso, who is Ed's mom. My hope is that you will be encouraged after reading about her life and the tremendous impact she has had on our family to live for the Lord.

You may think you do not currently have a generational blessing in your family lineage. However, the Lord wants you to know that you can be the one to change that. Or, if you are in a family that is already living out their calling as world changers, you can continue increasing the blessing that's already deposited there.

For a public speaking class, I had to choose someone I greatly admire and give a tribute speech about them, explaining why they are an extraordinary person. So, naturally, I decided to speak on my great-grandma who sadly passed away in 2017 at the age of 93.

Proverbs 10:7 says that a righteous man's memory will be a blessing, and this proved to be exceedingly true! The speech shared stories and qualities about her that defined her as the legacy she has become. I prayed beforehand that the Spirit would speak through me to give hope to the listeners, many of whom are in situations of true spiritual poverty. And the Lord did! I had many questions asked after speaking, classmates wanting to hear more about her and what it was that made her so loving and kind to others. And we all know what the answer to that is! God's Spirit is so real and present that even those who don't know or care about Him can feel it.

The reason I am telling you about this is because I want to encourage us to live a life so worthy of what God has called us to that our future great-grandchildren will be able to share glory stories that encourage future generations to continue in faith, and sow seeds of blessing and love! This can start with you. It is your choice. If your parents or grandparents or anyone in your family have never walked with the Lord, or even if they did, God is calling you to choose righteousness, and do so knowing how much it will bless your offspring one day.

It brings me so much joy to talk and hear about my Abuela. She was extraordinary on so many levels. Her physical and emotional strength exceeded that of most young people. Her positive, constantly optimistic attitude brought so much stability to those around her in hard times. She herself did not live an easy life by any means. She lived through pain and the loss of her mother at a young age, and later in life her husband, but by the grace of God she never let the devil draw her into self-pity or depression. She rose above and soared triumphantly on the wings of God's grace, and showed her children, grandchildren, and now great-grandchildren and those around them, how to live a humble life that serves the Lord in everything. For example, Abuela was a pastor's wife, she taught poor families how to feed themselves, she raised her six younger siblings when her mom died, defended herself from house intruders, she traveled internationally until the day she died, and so much more. I could go on and on!

Abuela was also an incredible cook. Her talent for making traditional Argentine food is to this day a blessing! I brought some homemade empanadas (a pastry she taught me and my sisters to make) to school when I gave the speech, and passed them out. Everyone was so excited about it, as you can imagine hungry college students would be, and God used it as a way to open their hearts to Him. This testifies that God can work through our talents when we ask Him to, even through food, as my grandma's book Food, Family, and Fun shows!

In conclusion, I feel so blessed to have had someone as amazing as my Abuela be my great-grandmother. She has helped to shape me into the person I'm becoming today. Her faith has inspired countless people, and I know it will continue to do so. I want to impart to you an Abuela anointing, that each and every one of your families will

ABUELA TERESA SILVOSO

receive a generational blessing. No matter where your family is at right now spiritually, God wants you to look above to Him, and see it the way that He does, full of hope and joy. God wants to and will bless and restore your family, and will use you, as soon as you let Him.

There is nothing I can add to this wonderful masterpiece. I encourage you to digest it, meditate on it, and then apply it!

28 THE TRANSFORMATIONAL OBEDIENCE OF A DAUGHTER

Our daughter Jesica was a freshman in high school who wanted to do something for Jesus. She went to our ministry offices and asked Ed, "Dad, can you give me something to do for the Lord?"

Ed replied, "Well, we are getting lots of requests for books and tapes. If you take charge of shipping them, it would be very helpful."

She told us later that she was hoping for something more "spiritual," but she obediently took over and developed our merchandise department, faithfully praying for every book and tape that went out, asking the Lord to bless the recipients.

One of the first shipments went to an inmate by the name of Sonny Lara at the San Quentin State Prison. The next one went to a bookstore in Ghana, Africa. Her acts of obedience set in motion a divine chain reaction that resulted in two cities being mightily impacted. Let me tell you about the first one.

A number of years after Jesica sent the materials to San Quentin, we heard Sonny share how the tapes he'd received from Jesica had blessed him while in prison. At the time, he was a new believer and the message of societal transformation touched him profoundly because he was a victim of the systemic evil prevailing in our cities, particularly in poor neighborhoods. So much so that before he was incarcerated as an adult, he had been in and out of Juvenile Hall more times than he cared to remember because of his involvement in gang crimes.

> Her acts of obedience set in motion a divine chain reaction that resulted in two cities being mightily impacted.

Once released from prison, he and his wife Linda planted a church in the roughest part of San Jose and began to minister to the local youth, mostly those involved in gang activities. Their church meets in a community center next to the park where gangs first started in the city. Today, that park is a safe place where parents spend time with their children. City officials appreciate the change in the neighborhood with awe mixed with perplexity because what once was the worst neighborhood where officers dreaded to patrol has now become a model of social transformation.

The congregation the Laras lead has become an Ekklesia[5], ministering not only to its members, but also to their neighbors. The fourth Sunday of each month, after the praise and worship, announcements and offerings are done, they lead the members to visit every home nearby. They knock on doors and kindly announce, "Since you couldn't come to Church today, we brought the Ekklesia to you! We want to make sure your needs are met, and we also want to pray for you."[6]

The seeds of faith for this transformational congregation were planted by the biblical teaching in the tapes that a young teenager, starting out in ministry, mailed to a prison in obedience to the Holy Spirit's leading. Amazing how much God does with what we place in His hands!

ELEGANT CHRISTMAS PARTY HOSTED BY THE LARAS NEAR THE PARK THAT ONCE WAS THE CONTROL CENTER FOR GANGS. MOST OF THE GUESTS RECEIVED CHRIST!

---

[5] The term *Ekklesia* used here and elsewhere in this book comes from Ed's book *Ekklesia: Rediscovering God's Instrument for Global Transformation* (Chosen, 2017).

[6] The full story is captured in a documentary available on the Transform Our World App that can be downloaded here: https://subsplash.com/transformourworld/app

29 GOD DID IT AGAIN

While developing our books and tapes department, Jesica asked the Lord where in Africa she should send a free copy of Ed's recently released book *That None Should Perish*. The Lord led her to send it to a bookstore in Ghana. At the time, Dave Carrol (a Canadian missionary) was serving there. One day he felt an urge to go to that bookstore to look for a book to read in English, and he bought the copy that had just arrived. In the book he learned about our ministry in Resistencia, Argentina, and particularly how prayer evangelism was used to change the spiritual climate over that city which resulted in tremendous church growth. He was encouraged and challenged by the book because he hadn't seen that kind of fruit in Africa, in spite of his efforts.

OUR GRANDSON EDAN BEING BAPTIZED AT THE PUBLIC BAPTISM IN HARMONY SQUARE IN BRANTFORD.

Upon his return to Canada, Dave told a pastor friend (Brian Beattie) how the book had inspired him. To his surprise, Brian told him that he had just read the same book and was looking for a way to put the principles into practice. This led to a partnership that changed the city of Brantford and has inspired other cities in Canada to launch similar transformation processes.

The heart of the story is found in the documentary entitled *Transformation in Brantford, Canada*[7], but let me give you the highlights:

Back in the 1990s, Brantford was considered one of the worst cities in Canada. Its downtown area was so dilapidated that a film producer chose it as the set for a horror movie. The place looked so bad that he didn't have to spend money staging it. Poverty, prostitution, drug addiction, unemployment and homelessness were prevalent.

After Brian and Dave applied the principles of prayer evangelism and transformation, things began to change rapidly. They bought a building that used to be a bar notorious

---

[7] The Brantford documentary can be purchased on DVD at transformationondemand.com/product/transformation-in-brantford-canada/

for the sinful acts that took place in it and turned it into a church. They adopted the crack houses in the surrounding area in prayer and ministered to drug dealers and drug addicts alike, sharing the love and the grace of God. Every weekend they served free hamburgers in the wee hours of the night to sinners coming out of houses of pleasure as a way to minister to them, especially to women. They organized cleaning crews and the area began to look better, but they also extended their outreach beyond that neighborhood.

They created a character called Captain Kindness (aka Dave Carrol) that taught school children the value of being kind and respectful. Teachers loved what Captain Kindness brought into the classroom and recommended it to other schools. Soon he was being invited to civic and official functions because the city felt that Captain Kindness was theirs. Many came to the Lord, including the mayor. The Member of Parliament (MP) representing Brantford made a motion in Parliament to declare Brantford the "Kindest City in Canada." What a change! Their church had become an Ekklesia because it began to do in the city what before was only done indoors.

CAPTAIN KINDNESS

When a local businessman who was involved in renovating the dilapidated downtown saw the positive impact this had on the city, he gave the church free space in his shopping plaza. They showed movies on the weekends to encourage the population to visit an area they had avoided before. Everybody was impressed by what they saw, new businesses were started and the economy improved.

> They began to do in the city what before was only done indoors.

The openness to the message of the Gospel increased, so Brian and Dave decided to hold public baptisms in the recently-constructed Harmony Square adjacent to a brand-new shopping center. Hundreds have been baptized there. They had so much favor with the city that they were asked to organize the "Frosty Fest" carnival every winter. They did such an excellent job that City Hall allowed them to also organize a Living Nativity every Christmas, an event that presents the Gospel to thousands every year.

Today, the pastor of that church, Brian Beattie, is a leader in our Transform Our World Network and the Director of Transformation Canada. Jesica's obedience—when she was just a freshman in high school—was used to put two men on a journey that is now touching a nation. How great is our God!

30 THE EKKLESIA BEGINS IN THE HOME

Shortly after God led Ed to publish his book *Ekklesia,* He prompted me to write *Food, Family and Fun.* I was so busy writing and trying to meet my deadlines that I did not realize until mine was published that our books complement each other perfectly. The following testimony by Pastor Cal Chinen of Hawai'i illustrates this so well:

In 2016, I was carefully reading Ed Silvoso's new book, Ekklesia, *and at the same time, I was preaching through the Epistle to the Ephesians. It was a perfect combination. With this new and wonderful illumination of the church that Ed was presenting, Ephesians and my understanding of the church was coming alive like never before. One of the key observations was that Jesus' Ekklesia, at its heart of hearts, is truly a family. "So now you Gentiles are no longer strangers and foreigners. You are citizens along with all of God's holy people. You are members of God's family (household, family member, οἰκεῖος)" (Ephesians 2:19; John 14:2). I repented before our congregation for treating it more like a business organization than a family—God's Family! It changed our congregation powerfully.*

But that was only the beginning of the huge paradigm shifts that God had in store for me. In the summer of 2016, Ed Silvoso called me and said, "Cal, Ruth is writing a book on our family. It looks like a cookbook, but it really is a book on the dynamics of our family. Would you be interested in taking an early look at it in the digital version before it is released? It is called Food, Family, & Fun.*"*

I immediately accepted Ed's offer. There was something about what Ed shared about Ruth's book that drew me. Ed and Ruth Silvoso have a wonderful marriage and family. It can be safely said that Ed almost never operates without Ruth. They are truly one in the Lord. Their love for each other is tangible. When you are in their presence, their love for each other spills over onto whoever is there with them. It is not the kind of love where one feels uncomfortable, but rather uplifted and blessed. And this dynamism and atmosphere increases if you are with them when they are with their children and grandchildren. It is like an overflowing fountain of God's honor, tenderness, and love.

As soon as I received the book, I began to read it. The more I read it, the more I realized that this was not just a book on how a loving, healthy, and powerful family operates, but it really was the powerful dynamic that Jesus' Ekklesia truly begins in the marriage and family. Too often, we have made a healthy congregation based on great principles but the family culture remains largely un-

changed. The church may grow and individuals may grow and change, but family dynamics and relationships remain the same. Ruth revealed the "secret sauce" of their marriage and family. It was not only a cookbook on how to make delicious meals, but also a cookbook on how to create healthy, loving, and impacting families. Ed Silvoso's book on the Ekklesia, together with Ruth's book, work perfectly together on how to create a healthy congregation starting with the family.

I was so moved by the simple but powerful lessons that Ruth talked about that I stopped the sermon series that I was on and taught a series based on the seven main points that Ruth shared in her book. Marriages and families were transformed as they practiced those seven principles. The incredible thing is that the same honor, tenderness, and love that I saw in the Silvoso Family was now seen growing in the families of

HAVING EKKLESIA TIME AT HOME WITH GRANDDAUGHTER ADDISON.

our congregation. Our own family was transformed and continues to be transformed! The sublime, beautiful and transformative power of the kingdom of God was released in the families of our congregation. The church is not only supposed to be a family, but every family is supposed to be an Ekklesia.

I have been a full-time pastor since 1980, but I have never seen so many families being transformed as I am seeing now. When a family realizes that it is called to be more than a family, it is called to be God's Ekklesia (which is really a family) with all the power and authority of God behind it, great things begin to happen. Brothers, sisters, parents, grandparents, husbands, and wives who could never get along with one another, much less talk with one another, do not have to stay that way. The power to bind and loose is given to Jesus' Ekklesia and, in the same way, it is given to a family who will choose to also be His Ekklesia. Marriages and families move from dysfunction to function, to transformative agents of God's Kingdom.

Ruth Silvoso has shown us the basic operative principles of her family, and in so doing has shown us the basic operative principles of a healthy, loving, and powerful family. In God's mysterious ways, could she also be showing us the basic operative principles for every healthy, loving, and powerful congregation? I believe she does!

Aloha,
Pastor Cal Chinen
Moanalua Gardens Missionary Church

This is why I love to say time and again that the Ekklesia begins in the home. Jesus said that when two or three gather in His name, He dwells in their midst. Imagine how empowering this can be for families: two or three, or more, with Jesus in their midst, doing what normally is done in a home–eating, playing, chatting, watching TV, texting–but with Jesus in their midst. How exciting!

Ed and I have made it a practice to continuously acknowledge the presence of Jesus in our home. We immediately felt the difference as soon as we did this, but those that visit us also feel it, even non-believers. It happened recently when a repairman came to fix something and "out of the blue" he exclaimed, "There is something different in this place. What is it?" It was so easy to share about Jesus because our home is an Ekklesia with Jesus in our midst.

I invite you to open the front door of your house, literally, and to welcome Him in. In Revelation 3:20, He assures us that He will be glad to come in and to fellowship with us if we hear His voice and open the door. What an exciting prospect to have Jesus living at home with us. Do it today!

THE KITCHEN IS THE HEART OF THE HOME.

31 HOME IS THE KEY

Home is so important because if things don't go well there, it's very hard to be successful at work or serving the Lord. Home is where everything significant starts and we all want to have a happy home.

Not too long ago, I watched an interview on TV featuring prominent figures in business and in the film industry. All of them were asked, "What is the most important thing in your life?"

Most of them answered, "My home—my family and children." Nobody said it was their next movie or business deal.

Today the family is under attack. Home is where memories are created, good and bad. We all know people who have a miserable life, and it usually goes back to a bad experience at home during their growing up years.

You might say, "I already messed up, my husband and I don't get along," or "My children are rebellious." Don't lose hope because the Lord can restore what the locust has eaten. He can take the broken pieces and make a beautiful new vessel. Even when our kids are older, they still need our prayers. Prayer is the key ingredient for a happy home. Make it a way of life. My mother was a woman of prayer. The day before she went to be with the Lord, she told us, "I am praying for each one of you." Those were her last words to us.

Ed's mother, before she went to heaven, also reminded us, "Keep serving the Lord always. There is nothing better in this life." Our parents were a great example to us.

Love is what holds a family together. Don't be afraid to demonstrate love in tangible ways to your spouse so your kids can see and envision a happy love life for themselves. It's better for them to learn romantic love from you than from TV or other media.

> Prayer is the best ingredient for a happy home. Make it a way of life.

Once we were ministering at a conference for top-level marketplace leaders on Ed's book Anointed for Business. Ed gave a very good presentation and before opening it up for questions he told a story from when he was a young new Christian.

EVEN OUR YOUNGEST GRANDDAUGHTER LYDIA UNDERSTANDS EKKLESIA!

There was a day when Ed's father scolded him in front of his friends for speaking negatively about their pastor, something he knew was against his father's rules. He was very hard on Ed. He scolded him and sent him to his room while his friends watched, but the next day he gathered all of the boys that had been there the night before and apologized to Ed while kneeling before him.

"What you did was wrong," his father said, "but what I did was worse. Will you forgive me, son?"

Ed says that his dad was never taller than the day he knelt down and apologized to him in front of his friends. What a powerful lesson.

After sharing this story in that meeting, a man sitting in the front row, clearly touched by it, started crying until his sobs became uncontrollable. Some of the people started ministering to him. Then, a lady raised her hand and said, "Can you tell me how I can minister to my family?" Another woman, seated next to me, leaned over and said, "Can you impart the anointing for my family to be restored, like you shared earlier on?"

These folks were attending a marketplace conference but they needed more help at home than at work. With so many needs at home, they found it difficult to work and minister freely. We ended up ministering to them about their greatest need, the family.

It is always helpful to remind ourselves that when people are facing eternity they do not ask for another day at the office. They want to see their loved ones.

Family is the key, and it is built one day at a time.

32 TRAIN UP A CHILD IN THE WAY SHE SHOULD GO

In *Food, Family and Fun* I teach that the family that eats, prays, ministers and plays to-gether *remains together*. Dinnertime is a perfect opportunity to do that on a daily basis.

Obviously, the eating part is very easy to implement since we all sit down to eat. Prayer also happens around the dinner table when we say grace. But, what about ministering during meal times? This is more difficult to grasp because we usually associate ministry with activities that we do in a church setting. We also do ministry outside the church, like when we go with our kids to summer camp or to Bible clubs. But is it possible to do ministry around the dinner table? Yes, and it is surprisingly easier than we may think. Let me share how we did it.

When our daughters were growing up, we wrote the names of all our neighbors on small cards and put them inside a jar that we kept on the dining room table. Every day the girls would take turns picking a name and leading in prayer for that particular person or family.

One day, when it was our daughter Jesica's turn, she picked a card with the name "Mr. B." We didn't know his full name because the day we moved in, he told us that he was "the neighborhood recluse" and didn't want to talk besides the initial welcome he was offering us that day. He said, "This is the only time you will hear from me. I leave early in the morning and come back late at night, and I don't enjoy talking to people."

Jesica prayed a very anointed prayer, asking specifically for the Lord to protect him. After the "Amen," she said, "I'm burdened for Mr. B. I feel that he is in danger and he lives all alone with no one to care for him. Can I write him a letter?" We agreed and she wrote this simple note with our address on the envelope and placed it in his mailbox:

Dear Mr. B,

I want you to know that our family prayed for your safety and protection tonight at dinnertime and we want you to know that Jesus loves you and so do we.

God bless you,

Jesica

Later that evening, there was a knock at the door. It was Mr. B with the letter in his hand, asking if there was someone named Jesica at this address. We invited him in and, deeply moved, he told us what had just happened to him.

There is a God, and He really does care for you.

While filling up his car with gas, a shooting broke out at the gas station. It was a very dangerous moment, with bullets flying and people ducking. When he was finally able to get away, he couldn't understand how he had escaped unharmed. On the way home, he was thinking that there must be a God because the fact that he was alive was nothing short of a miracle, and only God can perform miracles. His question was answered when he found that note from a junior high school student telling him that she had prayed for his protection. "Well," he said, "there must be a God after all because I should be dead right now."

"Yes," we told him, "there is a God, and He really does care for you!"

Mr. B saw the light of Christ that day as the fruit of our family ministry time around the dinner table which is evidence that it is possible to minister with your family during meals. I suggest that you incorporate ministry activities like this one into your dinner routine. You will see similar breakthroughs because, "The anxious longing of the creation waits eagerly for the revealing of the sons of God" (Romans 8:19). And it all began when we decided to eat, pray *and minister* while enjoying delicious food. It works!

33 THE BLESSING THAT KEEPS ON BLESSING

Now that our daughter Jesica has her own children (Melanie, Edan and Lydia), she and her husband Benjy have trained them in the way of the Lord, and as a result they continually see testimonies that build their faith, and the faith of their children, in addition to transforming their neighborhood. The following story is proof of that.

> Melanie prayed for her every day, and three months later God orchestrated a divine appointment to share the Gospel and lead her to the Lord.

Benjy and Jesica regularly prayer-walk their neighborhood with their kids, praying for every house they go by. Occasionally, they strike up a conversation with a neighbor and are able to pray for them and often meet their felt needs. On one particular day, they saw a young girl doing drugs at the park. At that moment, their daughter Melanie, moved by the spiritual need of this girl as evidenced by her desperation and addiction, heard the Holy Spirit prompt her to adopt the girl in prayer, to intercede faithfully for her salvation, and to buy her a Bible in faith that she would one day encounter and receive the love of Jesus.

Melanie shared this with her parents and they immediately bought a Bible as a prophetic act that one day they would be able to give it to the girl. Melanie wrote the date they had spiritually adopted her on the inside cover, she prayed for her every day, and three months later God orchestrated a divine appointment to share the Gospel and to lead her to the Lord. Melanie retrieved the Bible and showed her the date and the inscription. The young girl was blown away, moved to tears and deeply touched that someone had adopted her in prayer and bought a Bible for her in faith.

Benjy and Jesica began discipling and mentoring the girl, and teaching her the Word of God. A few years later, she passed away unexpectedly, but as Melanie put it, "I'm glad I obeyed the Holy Spirit because now I know she is in heaven with Jesus." The story doesn't end there, though. The girl's family asked Benjy to conduct her funeral and to share the Gospel, and many of her friends and family were able to hear the Good News for the first time and receive the love of Jesus!

After the funeral, Jesica and Benjy continued to adopt this household in prayer, caring for them and helping to meet some of their tangible felt needs. A few months later, they were able to lead the girl's mother to the Lord, and when she passed away recently, the family again asked Benjy to conduct the funeral and share the Gospel. Those in attendance were able to hear about Jesus and receive His love as well.

There is so much power in prayer walking and adopting our neighborhoods in prayer.

It's amazing to see how much eternal fruit came out of a very simple act of obedience when Jesica, as a junior high student, felt led to pray for Mr. B…and today her children follow in her footsteps. Begin to do it with your family; the rewards in heaven are eternal and the satisfaction on earth is enormous.

THE MACNAUGHTONS—JESICA, BENJY AND THEIR CHILDREN LYDIA, EDAN AND MELANIE —HAVE TURNED THEIR HOME INTO AN EKKLESIA.

34 COOKING UNDER THE ANOINTING

Every homemaker can have a "captive audience" at dinnertime if they make it a fun and pleasant occasion. Kids may not pay attention to our requests for attention or physical presence all day long until…dinnertime. That is when inevitably they come to the table because if they don't eat…they will die, to put it simply. There is no need to create a market for eating. The demand will always be there. So, let's take advantage of that immutable reality and turn it into a life-changing occasion.

To make the most of that opportunity, the concept of "cooking under the anointing" came to my mind, based on Paul's command in Colossians 3:23-24, "Whatever you do, do your work heartily, as for the Lord rather than for men, knowing that from the Lord you will receive the reward of the inheritance." What better reward can we receive on earth than building life-giving ties with family members, and more precisely, with our children during meal times?

Granted, they are not always the friendliest audience, especially when they enter the teen years, and the new complexities of life they face may lead them to question our authority or our wisdom. More devastating yet is when they turn away from the Lord. What can we do to bring them back? Or how can we lead an unbelieving family member to the Lord who gets upset, even violent, if we bring up the subject of the Gospel?

You can win them over without words simply by "cooking under the anointing"!

What do I mean by this? How can meals make a difference in the lives of people who are spiritually sick, or worse yet, oppressed by evil forces that blind them to the light of the Gospel?

We get an illuminating example in Acts 19:11: "God was performing extraordinary miracles by the hands of Paul, so that handkerchiefs or aprons were even carried from his body to the sick, and the diseases left them and the evil spirits went out."

Paul was making tents, and something divinely powerful was transferred from him to those garments so that when put in contact with spiritually needy people, they were set free. If God was able to use a handkerchief or an apron in biblical times to do that, He can also use a meal today cooked unto the glory of God and brought to the table to bless those in need of His blessing.

> If God was able to use a handkerchief or an apron in biblical times... He can use a meal cooked unto the glory of God.

I realize that this may sound strange and out of the ordinary. This is why the Bible describes what took place through Paul as "extraordinary miracles." In fact, it was no different than when people—like the woman with the issue of blood—touched Jesus' garment and got cured. Or when Peter's shadow came upon those lined up on the sidewalks of Jerusalem and healed them. Or the passage in the Old Testament that describes how a corpse was accidentally dropped on a prophet's grave, touched the dry bones of the servant of God and came back to life. Strange? Yes. True? Of course, since it is written in the Book. Extraordinary? Absolutely.

In light of those biblical examples—anointed garments that heal and deliver people from ailments or demonic oppression, shadows that cure the sick, and dry bones that upon contact resurrect people—the concept of "cooking under the anointing" doesn't seem so radical. By this I mean chopping the onions in the Name of the Lord, frying the hamburgers seasoned with prayers of blessing, doing it all heartily, as unto the Lord, expecting to receive a reward from Him.

One woman who heard me speak about "cooking under the anointing" decided to try it. This is what she told me afterward:

> *I was having a real problem with my teenage son. There was constant tension because he had become very rebellious. We found ourselves arguing all the time about many things, but what really triggered things was that his room was always a mess. I scolded him for it and tried every way I could to convince him that he should at least make his bed. It got so bad that finally I threatened, "If you don't make your bed, don't come to dinner." But he continued to disobey. Since dinner was already cooked and served, I had to let him eat but his disobedience and my anger turned the dinner table into a war zone.*
>
> *After I heard Ruth speak about "cooking under the anointing," I decided to try it. I chose to bless him rather than blast him. The Lord worked in my own life first; he showed me how to forgive, bless and love him more. I also made it a practice to pray for him while I cooked, and I prayed over the food as I prepared it and when I brought it to the table. Even though he still didn't make his bed, much less clean his room, at least this improved the atmosphere during dinner considerably. It changed from a war to a truce.*

However, after cooking under the anointing for a while, one day, when I called my son to dinner, he said, "Mom, before we eat, I want to show you something in my room." I had been avoiding his room so I wouldn't lose my determination to overlook his disobedience, but when I got there...I couldn't believe my eyes. He had not only made his bed, but he had cleaned the room and put everything in its place! We hugged and cried...what a transformation!

Cooking under the anointing happens when the kitchen becomes a habitat of the Holy Spirit and everything we do there is done as unto the Lord: cooking a meal, making a cup of tea, whatever it is, always giving thanks to God and blessing the family. This is how I apply Colossians 3:23 in my kitchen. Try it. It works!

35 BRING GOD INTO THE KITCHEN AND CHANGE YOUR FAMILY

Home is where our most intimate and sensitive memories are created, both good and bad. Unfortunately, the bad ones often turn into chains that hold us back from achieving the destiny that God has for us, but the Lord is willing and able to make "all things"—good and bad—work together for good because nothing is impossible for Him.

Ellie Kapihe is a Samoan pastor in Honolulu, Hawaii. Samoans are warm and beautiful people who traditionally struggle with anger, often expressed in harsh physical punishment of children by the head of the household. Such was the case in Ellie's family until God intervened to turn the broken pieces into one of His *masterpieces*. The following is Pastor Ellie's story of how God changed his life, as well as his family's, when he began to "cook under the anointing" after he heard the principles I share in my book *Food, Family and Fun*:

The Lord directed me to purchase two cast iron skillets and told me that these were the instruments He was going to use to bring reconciliation to our family, especially with our oldest daughter, Teila. My anger, acting as a very powerful stronghold that I was unable to control in those days, created separation between me and my daughter, which eventually had a very negative effect on our whole family. The Lord pointed out to me that because of my inability to discipline my children with love, gentleness and kindness, they lived in constant fear and were afraid of being near me.

However, from that day on, each time I cooked for my family, the Lord led me to use that time to pray for them. I was directed to cook the food as an act of worship unto the Lord and intercession for my family. As I did that over each meal, the Lord began to touch and eventually He changed my heart because when I was praying for the family, the Holy Spirit came upon me each time. I began to confess my lack of self-control and repent of my hurtful ways that had resulted in isolation from my loved ones. The Lord deeply ministered to me while I was cooking; it was as if my heart, mind and whole being were going through transformation in the kitchen. In fact, the kitchen had become an altar on which the presence of God dwelt. This resulted in the food being blessed and becoming a vehicle to bless others.

When I brought the food cooked under the anointing and guidance of the Holy Spirit to the table, our family was finally able to eat in peace and we began to share personal things with one another. For the first time, we were really listening to each other. In the beginning, we didn't share any deep issues, but we definitely felt that we were moving closer to one another which felt so good after years of isolation. Over time, we came to share more intimate things, even outside of the mealtimes through Holy Spirit orchestrated "appointments."

I discovered that the Lord used the time I dedicated to Him while cooking meals to plant seeds for our family to eat in peace, which then opened doors for connectedness. Today, we are closer than ever, learning more and more how to confide in each other and build one another up to become the family that God designed us to be. Peace, joy and freedom are the result of bringing things into the light of God's presence that now dwells in the kitchen and around the dinner table as much as it does in a church building.

What an inspiring story! God indeed loves families and He is ready and eager to restore and transform them. Nothing is impossible for Him. No matter how much the evil one may have defiled your family, God is in the restoration business.

Dedicate yourself to the Lord and follow His lead. Even a cup of water given in the name of the Lord can become a vehicle to touch others with God's love. How much more a meal cooked unto His glory!

THIS PHOTO OF WAIKIKI BEACH IN HONOLULU WAS TAKEN BY OUR GRANDSON MAX.

PART 3

FAITH-BUILDING STORIES FROM AROUND THE WORLD

In Part 3, I share testimonies from all over the globe.

Most of these stories feature Christian leaders who Ed and I have the privilege and joy of leading in transformation. Many consider themselves our spiritual children — even though some are older than us. The reason for this goes back to 2007 when God showed us that our ministry should be a family and not just an organization.

This new understanding radically changed not only how we interact with them, but how they relate to each other and to the congregations and businesses they lead. But above everything else, it highlights the importance of the church being anchored in homes and in families.

36 ALL RISE... THE HONORABLE LORD JESUS PRESIDING

Hong Kong became a British Colony in 1842, and as a result it became Western in outlook, business practices and education, while maintaining its rich Chinese language, roots and heritage. Barbara Chan, a Judge in the District Court of Hong Kong, heard the transformation message for the first time when we went there in the mid 1990s. Those were days of growing uncertainty as the United Kingdom was finalizing arrangements to return control of the colony to Communist China. Because of that, we proceeded to generate intercession for the upcoming transfer. We were led by the Lord to generate one million hours of intercession through our network of pastors and intercessors in Argentina.

Through this exercise, Hong Kong and Argentina became linked in the heavenly places in a most powerful and inspiring way. A businesswoman who attended our transformation conference donated $100,000 to our ministry and we decided to use that money to scholarship 1,000 pastors to our conference in Mar del Plata, Argentina. As this began to unfold, we were blessed by reports of people in Argentina, especially in remote areas, praying for a place that was on the opposite side of the world with fervor and passion. And it worked...because we reached the one million mark and the transition of Hong Kong back to China took place peacefully. We remember the joy that invaded everyone that year at our international conference in Mar del Plata when we introduced the delegation from Hong Kong to those 1,000 pastors! Everybody was touched and many were moved to tears. Among those was Barbara Chan who became a close ministry associate and eventually our ministry leader in the region. The following story is how Barbara turned her courtroom into an Ekklesia:

> *When I was a judge in the District Court of Hong Kong, I was blessed by the ministry and teaching of the Silvosos, in particular Ed's teaching in his book* Anointed for Business. *Although I had been serving God through my work when I was a lawyer, becoming part of the team of Transform Our World brought me to another level of understanding as to how to live in the power and the presence of God in the courtroom. Every day as I prepared for my cases for the next day, I prayed for the parties of the case, the lawyers and for their circumstances. Also, in the course of the hearing I would continue to pray. One of the most difficult parts of a judge's work is to determine when witnesses are telling the truth and when they are lying. The Holy Spirit taught me to bind the demonic spirits that cause people to tell lies in the name of Jesus and I began to do that every day in my courtroom.*

One day, I was hearing a case that related to a contract debt. The defendant who owed the debt had filed a defense stating that there were defects in the goods sold to him. As usual, I prayed for the parties and I bound the demonic spirits that caused witnesses to tell lies and forbade them to operate in my courtroom. During the course of the hearing, when the plaintiff was giving evidence, I noticed that the defendant looked very uneasy and nervous. I thought it related to the fact that he did not have the money to pay for the contract debt. I began to pray for him and to bless him under my breath. The more I prayed for him, the more uneasy he looked.

After the plaintiff had given evidence, the defendant came to the witness box. He stood up to swear to tell the truth. The usual step to take after swearing is that the witness sits down to begin his testimony. However, after he sat down, instead of beginning his testimony, he said, "Your Honor, give judgment against me!" I was surprised at that unprecedented action, totally out of the ordinary, and I asked what he meant. He again said, "Give judgment against me!" One more time, I asked what he meant as he had filed a defense and at the start of the trial he had also said that he was defending the claim. He just said, "Give judgment against me!"

Eventually, I began to understand that he had been so convicted by the Holy Spirit that he could not lie anymore in my courtroom, and he decided that instead of defending his case, he would ask for judgment to be entered against him. I realized that the more I prayed for him, the more convicted he became. I knew that he could make an application to the court for payment of the judgment debt in installments, and I advised him as he did not have a lawyer to help him with that.

A CARICATURE OF BARBARA CHAN IN THE COURTROOM

After judgment was rendered against him, and following the advice I gave him, I saw relief on his face. I know that the Lord was in the case because He loves this defendant and He wanted him to face up to his responsibilities. Also, I knew the power of prayer and the authority of the Ekklesia to bind and loose, and that authority is so great that it can stop the demonic spirits from operating in a courtroom and can also bring people to tell the truth!

What a stirring example of how to take the power and the presence of God to the workplace. In fact, one day we received a call from Barbara Chan to inform us that she had just invited a pastor to baptize a judge in chambers! He had come to faith through her applying prayer evangelism to his situation! If God can do it in a courtroom, He can do it in your place of work, too.

37 UGANDA, AFRICA: THE FRUIT OF BLESSING A MUSLIM MAYOR

We visited Uganda in 2009 and had the opportunity to meet and minister to the First Lady, a wonderful Christian woman. She attended our seminar on transformation with her entourage that also included a fierce looking, machine gun touting security detail.

We were very impressed by her humility, and once we spent some private time with her, by her deep spirituality. She was definitely an intercessor. The following year she came to Mar del Plata, Argentina, to attend our Global Conference on Transformation. With her came cabinet members and family members, including her nephew Joseph Okia, a medical doctor who also serves as an advisor to the President.

The story he tells below illustrates the power of blessing based on Jesus' teachings in Luke chapter 10. This principle was tested to the limit because the newly elected mayor of Kampala, the capital of Uganda, was very corrupt. He had served time in prison for fraud and it was widely believed that his election had been tainted by corruption. Christians were appalled that a Muslim—and a corrupt one—was in charge of the city. They felt powerless until...well, read the story. It is fascinating!

> *The transformation principles that we have learned from Ed and Ruth are not mere philosophies or biblical exposition. They are truths that when put into action yield powerful and tangible results. They always exhort us to bless, fellowship, minister to felt needs and proclaim the kingdom. This is Prayer Evangelism, a scriptural approach taken from the book of Luke, where Jesus exhorts us to "speak peace" (Luke 10:5), "stay in one place, eating and drinking (fellowship – Luke 10:7), "heal the sick" (minister to the felt needs – Luke 10:9) and to "proclaim the Kingdom of God" (Luke 10:9).*

> *God taught us in a profound manner the incredible power of speaking peace to our circumstances, to our cities and to our nation.*

> *In 2007, as a group of believers in the city of Kampala, the capital city of Uganda, we started crying out for transformation. The city was a chaotic patchwork of pot-holed streets, made worse by torrential tropical rain storms that filled the pot-holes to lake-like dimensions. Originally built for 100,000 inhabitants, the rapid population expansion had swelled the city's numbers to over four million people. A corrupt city council had long abandoned the idea of garbage collection, or any other municipal service for that matter, and was more content to fraudulently parcel out vacant*

city land and houses among a small group of connected cronies. Garbage filled the streets and the entire city was groaning for redemption.

At first our prayers were filled with anger and frustration. Could not God intervene in the misfortunes of our city? What was required for God to do so? We prayed in anger, but there was no answer, for God desires for men (and women) everywhere to lift up holy hands without anger and without dissension (see 1 Timothy 2:8).

Finally, God spoke to us.

"You must repent to the mayor. You must bless the City. Repent of your anger!"

That was not the message we wanted to hear. But obedience is better than sacrifice and so, begrudgingly, we obeyed.

JOSEPH OKIA

A call was placed to the mayor's office asking for an appointment to see him. Several weeks later we had our appointment. The mayor, a muslim and convicted felon, was certainly not the kind of person we expected to bless, but there the biblical mandate was clear: speak peace and bless your enemies, start with blessing, because blessing is more powerful than cursing and Ed and Ruth have always reminded us of the biblical truth, "The God of peace will soon crush Satan under your feet" (Romans 16:20).

When we arrived, the entire city council was assembled. Directors, city managers, enforcement officers and prominent businessmen were all looking at this small bunch of Christians, wondering what would happen next.

"Your Excellency, the Mayor, we want to repent. Our Bible tells us to pray for those in authority (1 Timothy 2:1), and yet we have not prayed for you, but against you. In doing so we have cursed you and spoken ill of you. We repent; will you forgive us?"

A stunned silence filled the room. What would this muslim mayor do?

He lifted his hands to the heavens and shouted: "Praise the Lord! Please pray for me!"

At that precise moment the presence of God invaded the Town Hall as everyone, the entire municipal council, raised their hands to the Lord! Muslims, Catholics, and Christians from all denominations eagerly muttered "Amen" as we prayed for them and blessed them! Hallelujah, what a moment.

So, what was the result of speaking a blessing over the mayor, a Muslim?

Within weeks the government announced a major plan to overhaul the road network in the city. All traffic intersections were remodeled and upgraded with the latest traffic lights and modern street lighting. Even the potholes were fixed!

A forensic audit of the city's finances uncovered over $20 million US dollars in hidden slush funds that were now re-channeled in rebuilding the city. A brand-new garbage collection system was introduced and the city is now clean, swept and without rubbish. The mayor joined hundreds of believers in declaring Kampala the City of God. The municipal council embarked on a major revamp of its brand and image that saw the city reborn as a model in transparency and financial accountability, winning national and international awards! The power of blessing broke the curse over the city and allowed God to move in, and when God moves in, darkness has to flee!

Time and again we have seen how blessings break the power of curses. This is because a blessing is empowered by Jesus, whereas a curse has its source in the devil, the one defeated at Calvary.

We have turned this principle into a lifestyle, and as a result we have seen people that used to annoy us with their unkindness, even hurt us with their meanness, radically transformed. We have witnessed the spiritual climate change for good in our neighborhood after we began to prayer walk, speaking peace upon every household.

If God was able to inject transformation into a corrupt government and a dilapidated city in Africa, He can certainly change everything in your sphere of influence. Let's stop blasting and begin to bless, and we'll see the spiritual climage change for the better.

38 ABERDEEN, SCOTLAND: REDIGGING WELLS OF REVIVAL

In 1997, we led a mission trip to the northeast of Scotland. We took a group with people from California, Canada and Argentina. Most of them were young and beginners in ministry, so we trained them in the mornings and we sent them all over the city in the afternoons to visit homes, minister on the streets and in parks, perform skits and drama to draw attention for them to preach to those that would gather. It's fair to say that the whole city was saturated with the Gospel. Everybody heard about Jesus. We even marched with the Salvation Army Band on the streets. It was wonderful.

At night we had a big tent where we would preach and feature fresh testimonies of the things that happened during the day. After the evening meetings, we set up a place downtown and offered free coffee and snacks that the local ladies prepared. Everyone was witnessing to those that came in. I made Argentinean empanadas, too, and we had awesome testimonies from that outreach. Here's one:

A young, good-looking man came by with several friends. The group from Argentina started talking to him about God but he was resisting. Finally, they asked him, "What would it take for you to believe in Jesus?"

To this he replied, "If my sister gets healed, I will believe. She is blind and has diabetes." They told him, "Bring her here."

> He brought her, our team prayed for her, and she was healed instantly!

He brought her, our team prayed for her, and she was healed instantly! The young man accepted Jesus and we learned that he was the drug dealer of the city. Those that came with him also received Jesus. When we visited that city again several years later, I asked about him and was glad to learn that he was serving in leadership at one of the local churches.

This is a wonderful story and we saw many lives touched, but that trip also impacted those that went with us to minister. A teacher who was part of our team told me recently that the trip radically changed her life because she saw miracles and experienced the presence and the power of God like never before.

For me and Ed, along with our children, ministering in Scotland was very special because the United Kingdom was used by God to send missionaries to Argentina. That is how my parents met Jesus. This trip was like redigging those wells of revival. As Ed told them on the opening night, "We did not come to teach you something new, but simply to remind you of what your missionaries taught us."

39 IRELAND: HEARTS ARE BEING TRANSFORMED

CLIFFORD SULLIVAN

Our dear friend, Clifford Sullivan, a respected lawyer in Dublin, Ireland, wrote this testimonial about transformation in Ireland and the role our family, by the grace of God, has had in it. He writes:

Transformation is happening in Ireland. Hearts are being transformed.

Ed and Ruth Silvoso have always emphasized that transformation must happen in us before we see transformation happen around us. At the Transform Our World Global Conference some years ago, Ed spoke passionately of the need for a fresh Holy Spirit baptism of love and compassion for those outside of our theological, social, or cultural ponds. I was changed where I sat. How narrow my thinking had been, and how far from the heart of God who so loves the world, all of it and everyone in it. The Holy Spirit circumcised my heart. I felt something of what Peter, as recorded in Acts 10, must have felt when instructed to go to Cornelius' house. A Gentile! Really, God? But out of Peter's obedience and change of heart, the first Gentiles came to faith in Jesus and the Holy Spirit fell on them. A rock had been hurled into the pond of Peter's theological and social worldview. It created more than a ripple; it was a tsunami. Nothing was ever the same again. In my life and in the Transform Our World grouping in Ireland, we have been experiencing that too.

All the "them-and-us" attitudes that separate the people of God from the people God wants to touch through us, have to go. We have seen Ed and Ruth bring reconciliation between First Nations and colonizers, between Afro-American and white peoples and, inspired by this, we sought God about the deep divisions in our own land, and God has opened up doors of reconciliation in our nation.

Ireland has been ravaged by religious and political division for centuries. Ed's Ekklesia message has enabled us to embrace our brothers and sisters in Christ across denominational and sectarian divides. Ancient dividing walls, that gave the devil jurisdiction, are coming down between Catholic and Protestant, between Ireland and England. Due to our history, the deep wounds of religious division may be more particular to Ireland than other countries, but in every country, similar wounds are also felt at social and cultural levels. This circumcision of our hearts allows us to touch people who don't share our worldview. The disciples were surprised at the engagement by Jesus with the

Samaritan woman at the well, but this opened up her entire village to believe—so transformation will often happen in unexpected settings.

Communities in Ireland are being touched as they experience new levels of grace and peace from us. Inspired by Prayer Evangelism, a local church has become integrated into an inner-city Dublin community that is both socially and economically deprived, and people are experiencing from us non-judgmental love and kindness. As a result, people are opening their hearts to a God whose Ekklesia cares for them, accepting them as they are and who they are. The City authorities have noticed and have given the church an award for outstanding contribution to the community and are investing millions of euro to transform the lives of this community.

Most of all, Ed and Ruth model what they teach us. I have been inspired by observing their marriage and family life. Likewise, their hunger and thirst for more and more of the Spirit. Their ministry brings out in and through us dimensions of the Kingdom of God and encourages us on to be more than we would otherwise be. We are profoundly grateful to God and so appreciative of them both.

Ireland is one of the most picturesque places on earth and its people are among the nicest in the world. To see the beginning of transformation in a nation is so encouraging!

40 HONG KONG: EKKLESIA IN THE FASHION INDUSTRY

On one of our ministry trips to Hong Kong, Mimi Chan, a friend and co-worker in our network (Transform Our World), invited us to lunch. It was refreshing to spend time with her and her husband Y.K. because they were applying in their family and business the principles of *Prayer Evangelism* and *Anointed for Business* that Ed teaches. The elegant lunch was catered at her fashion "Atelier" because she wanted us to pray and anoint her business. The name of her company is Milagros, which is very appropriate because it means *miracles* in English.

Mimi is very well-known and highly respected in the fashion industry because of the excellence of her work and the exquisite products she supplies to industry leaders to whom she also ministers.

On that particular day, there was a group of influential designers, models and professional photographers who had come from New York working in one of her rooms. They had come to solicit her services, for which they had

MIMI CHAN

MIMI WITH DAUGHTER CAMELLIA AND MANAGEMENT TEAM

suggested a certain time slot. When she heard about it, Mimi said, "You'll need to wait for me until I'm free because my spiritual parents are coming to pray for my business and to bless this place."

The group was first intrigued, and then interested by this, and after Mimi elaborated further, they asked if Ed and I could bless them, too. When we met them, the depth of their spiritual hunger impressed us. They immediately suspended the photo shoot that was going on and hung on every word and gesture of ours as we explained that God loves not just people but the world, which includes the marketplace. They had never pictured Jesus, or His apostles, running businesses, or heard about Dorcas (who I believe was a designer) or Lydia, a supplier of top-level materials, all of whom became leaders in the Church in the book of Acts.

They had never pictured Jesus, or His apostles, running businesses.

Those examples spoke powerfully to them because those are biblical characters that were involved in the business they are in today. We noticed some of them holding back tears. Such is the power of the Word of God. When we prayed, they felt the presence of God and that opened the door for us to point them to the redemptive work of Jesus at the Cross. It was a divine appointment and their respect for Mimi increased exponentially, widening the door for her to continue to witness to them.

For us, it was very encouraging to see how God is using Mimi. She has converted her business into an Ekklesia and is taking the Kingdom of God to an industry that influences the whole world. God is at work in the marketplace, including your own place in it. Be encouraged!

MIMI MINISTERING IN HER ATELIER

41 UKRAINE: THE WIDOW'S MITE REENACTED

One afternoon I was going through the drawers in my desk looking for a document, and came across a journal I used to keep. As I perused it, I saw what I had written about our ministry trip to the Ukraine in the late 1990s. I'm including it in this book because it's very moving and inspiring.

We were ministering on a Sunday at a church in Kiev, the capital, and there was a cute girl seated behind us that kept looking at me. She was shy and nervous, holding something very tightly in her hand.

When the pastor told the people, "Go and greet someone with the love of the Lord," she came running up to me, hugged me, and gave me the money that she had been holding in her hand. I thanked her and hugged her back.

The pastor's wife—seated next to me—told me that her name was Ivana, and that the amount she had given me (the equivalent of five U.S. dollars) was her monthly salary.

I went looking for her at the end of the service, hugged and prayed for her and thanked her again. At that moment, I could have returned the money, but if I had, I would have deprived her of the joy of giving, and denied her the blessings that God promises to a cheerful giver. I think of Ivana often, and when I do, I pray for her and ask God to bless her for her generosity.

> "Truly I say to you, this poor widow put in more than all the contributions to the treasury..."

This experience reminds me of a teaching I read somewhere about the story of the widow's mite, of her gift to God, told in the Gospels of Mark and Luke. I'm afraid I don't recall who wrote it or where I saw it, but this is how I remember it: Jesus was with His disciples, watching people depositing money into the offering receptacles. He watched as the rich were putting large sums of money, until a widow came along with just two small coins in her hand. They were the smallest coins and worth very little. The widow put them in the box and Jesus called His disciples over to point out, "Truly I say to you, this poor widow put in more than all the contributors to the treasury; for they all put in out of their surplus, but she, out of her poverty, put in all she owned, all she had to live on" (Mark 12:43-44; Luke 21:1-4).

There are several things this story teaches us:

1. *God sees what man overlooks.*

The big gifts in the Temple were surely noticed by people. That is probably what the disciples were paying attention to, but Jesus saw what no one else did; He saw the humble gift of a poor widow. This was the gift that Jesus considered worthy of comment. This was the gift that the disciples needed to be aware of. The other gifts made a lot of noise as they jingled into the receptacles, but the widow's mites were heard in heaven.

2. *God's evaluation is different than that of man.*

The rich were giving large sums of money, but they still retained their fortunes. The widow "put in all she owned, all she had to live on." Hers was a true sacrifice.

3. *Giving to God in the midst of our own need is an expression of faith.*

This woman was in need of charity herself, yet she had a heart to give. The amount was insignificant; what could she buy with it? She gave it in faith that God could use it, and by faith she gave the last of her money.

Like the widow who gave her last meal to Elijah in 1 Kings 17:7-16, we can be certain that she was provided for. God always provides for our needs (Matthew 6:25-34).

Jesus commented on the scribes who "devour widows' houses," religious officials of the day who instead of helping those in need, were content to rob them. The system was corrupt and the darkness of the scribes' greed makes the widow's sacrifice shine even more brightly.

4. *When it comes to giving at the church, God doesn't look at what we give but at what we keep.*

He really values when we give Him everything as an expression of faith that He can return it many times over, and in the process multiply it to bless others as Jesus did with the loaves and the fish the young lad gave him.

"God loves a cheerful giver" (2 Corinthians 9:7) because giving blesses us, blesses those that will benefit from the gift, and blesses God as He sees how we emulate Him who gave us His very best in Jesus Christ.

KIEV, UKRAINE

42 PHILIPPINES: CITIES AND MONEY DEDICATED TO GOD

When we built the prayer chapel in Argentina, at a time of great physical and financial weakness due to Ed's illness, we never imagined how much God was going to use and multiply that seed as you will see in the story shared below by Ricardo "King" Flores, our director in the Philippines.

Ed's first book *That None Should Perish* chronicled God's mighty work in Resistencia when the church discovered and implemented prayer evangelism, making that city an icon for city transformation.

KING FLORES

Right after it was published, King got hold of a copy of Ed's book in Singapore (it was not yet available in the Philippines), made a few photocopies, and studied it with a group of Christians that were hungry to see something similar happen in their nation. King told us jokingly afterward that the way Filipinos understood the meaning of the term *copyright* is "You have the right to copy it as long as you copy it *right.*"

They were so inspired by the stories in that book and so empowered by the biblical principles behind the stories that they invited us to visit Manila. We were deeply moved when we saw the original "copy" of the book that looked like a papyrus excavated from an archeological site. It had been read and re-read by so many that rather than wrinkles, its pages had scars. They had passed it around to a countless number of avid readers because the book was not available in the Philippines and they couldn't afford to buy the version printed in the U.S. We were so moved by what we saw that we arranged with our publisher to have 15,000 copies of a special edition printed locally and sold for two dollars each.

It was a small beginning, but one that grew until not one, but many cities were reached for Christ. Rejoice as you read this report from King.

The transformation story of Parañaque City, Philippines, was an offshoot of the successful account of a motel chain once used for prostitution that became a godly, family-centered motel business using the principles of prayer evangelism that we learned from Ed and Ruth Silvoso in 1997.

During a big conference in Manila where they were sharing these principles with pastors and leaders, a city hall employee from Parañaque City, a suburb of Manila, who attended was touched by the message and started applying prayer evangelism at work. It was a very timely move because the newly elected mayor had inherited a one billion Filipino peso debt (approximately US$250 million) from his predecessor and the city could no longer pay the employees' salaries.

The first thing this person did when she went back to work was to open the door of City Hall and invite Jesus to come in, as taught in Revelation 3:20. Then she introduced herself to everybody as their pastor who would be praying for them and for that place. Christians who in the past had remained silent about their faith, began to identify themselves and to connect with each other. Shortly afterward, daily morning prayers were offered for the mayor to find a solution to the debt problem, which he willingly accepted. In two months' time, God answered those prayers when taxpayers supernaturally became convicted and started to pay back taxes. Over time, the annual collection grew from 900 million pesos to 4 billion pesos. As of this writing, the yearly budget for the city is 20 billion pesos.

Because the spiritual climate at city hall improved, corruption diminished significantly. Permits were released within a day without having to pay a bribe, endemic problems with garbage collection were solved, crime rates went down, an Ekklesia was planted inside city hall, and the mayor was recognized as the best mayor in the nation in just two years' time.

The biblical principle of praying for those in authority that we have learned is so powerful that the mayor dedicated the city to God and inscribed those words on our city seal. This created a chain reaction that impacted other institutions. The Chief Justice of our Supreme Court received the Lord and invited Jesus into the highest Tribunal in the nation. The Commander in Chief of the Army came to Christ and did the same for the Army. The Flag Officer of the Navy (the equivalent of the U.S. Chief of Naval Operations) dedicated that branch of the Armed Forces to the Lord. And the leaders of our central bank inserted a verse from the Bible on one of our bills that reads, "Blessed is the nation whose God is the Lord" (Psalm 33:12). This turned those bills into Gospel tracts that on a daily basis proclaim the Word of God. Since then, our country has stopped borrowing and started to lend to other nations.

We are so grateful to the church in Argentina, and particularly to Ed and Ruth Silvoso, for their faithfulness. We know the beginning of their ministry was not easy, but now we see fruit, much fruit, and fruit that is multiplied.

It is amazing and encouraging to see how much God can do through someone (King Flores and a city employee in this case) who wholeheartedly takes hold of biblical principles and implements them. An entire nation is being touched.

43 THAILAND: HOW REBUILDING A MUSLIM SCHOOL BROUGHT A PASTOR BEFORE THE KING

In Phuket, Thailand, the tsunami that devastated that nation in 2004 destroyed practically all the property facing the ocean, and quite a bit inland, too. Pastors Brian and Margaret Burton and their congregation worked tirelessly aiding the multitude of victims. Their church building became a field hospital. It was a major crisis and despite the incredible efforts of international aid agencies, the effects of the disaster were far greater than anything yet experienced.

One of the places destroyed by the tsunami was a Muslim school. Brian was asked by the Deputy Governor of Phuket to help out at Kamala, one of the worst affected villages on the island. As he stood on the beach where a school stood before the wave destroyed it completely, God spoke to him audibly, "Rebuild the school."

Brian didn't have the know-how or finances to do it, but he eventually surrendered to the Lord and said yes.

Before being called to Thailand, Brian was a school teacher in England. He drew on his experience as a teacher and drew a basic plan of his "ideal" school. He submitted the plan to the local authority for them to consider commissioning him to build the school, but he still had no money to fund it. This was a problem as several large international corporations had also submitted plans to build the school and they had ample financial clout.

BRIAN BURTON

Brian had done all that was humanly possible, but his business partner in the project was God. A few weeks passed and Brian received a phone call asking him to report to the King's Palace in Bangkok to discuss his proposal. The King of Thailand himself was impressed by the design and Brian was commissioned to raise the funds to build the school.

The Royal Thai Engineers would carry out the construction, but on his return to Phuket he still faced the overwhelming obstacle of not having the money to finance the project. Standing on the beach, Brian cried out to God, "What shall I do?"

At that moment someone tapped him on the shoulder and Brian turned around to see a reporter from the BBC asking if she could interview him about the school. Brian saw a God-given opportunity and made an appeal which went nationwide in the UK. That wasn't all…after the BBC reporter had finished, a reporter from CNN stepped up, then the New York Times…and so on and so on.

People donated money from 42 different nations of the world and in two weeks they had enough for the whole project. Later that year, Brian was asked to go to the King's Palace and received a medal for his part in the Tsunami relief.

SCHOOL BUILT BY PASTOR BRIAN BURTON

Some may wonder, what is the spiritual fruit of an evangelical missionary rebuilding a Muslim school? Well, among other things, for several years Brian was invited to teach at that school on the work of Christ during Easter and Christmas. The Word was being planted and watered in the lives of young people who otherwise might never know about the loving God who gave His life for them.

That wasn't the only miracle. In another province further north, a fishing village was hit by the tsunami, all the houses and fishing boats were destroyed and people were left hungry and destitute. In addition, they became terribly afraid of the ocean which until then had been their main source of support. Brian and his team visited the village and led all the villagers to Christ on January 6, 2005, as a result of meeting their felt needs. Pastor Brian began to minister to these babies in Christ who were in dire need of wood to rebuild their boats.

No wood was available because the existing stock had been completely used up. Brian prayed with these new Christians and encouraged them to believe that God would make a way where there seemed to be no way.

Because the locals were afraid of the ocean, Brian decided to set up his tent between them and the water and went to sleep. In the middle of the night he was awakened by a. commotion outside his tent. The locals were shouting ecstatically, "Wood is raining from heaven! Come and see, Pastor!"

> The Word was being planted in the lives of young people who otherwise might never know about the loving God who gave His life for them.

When Brian came out of the tent, he indeed saw wood falling out of the sky. In the morning, they saw seven neat piles of wood, pre-cut and ready to be assembled into boats. At first, no one could believe it, but the evidence was right there. It had to be God! In no time, they built new boats and were once again fishing without any fear of the water because a truly extraordinary miracle had set them free.

This story, as unbelievable as it may seem to us today, is no different than the ones we read about in the Bible. A miracle is a divine intervention in human affairs to reveal His love and power to us. It can happen again because "Jesus Christ is the same yesterday and today and forever" (Hebrews 13:8).

IT WAS A MIRACLE THAT WOOD WAS PROVIDED SO SUPERNATURALLY BUT AN EVEN MORE EXTRAORDINARY MIRACLE THAT IT WAS PRE-CUT AND READY TO BE ASSEMBLED.

44 THAILAND: WOMEN ARISING AND SHINING

Margaret Burton sent me this wonderful story about how *Food, Family and Fun* is helping her raise up women to be transformation agents in Thailand.

In March 2012, I founded a Transformation Women's ministry (Destiny) in our church, Phuket Christian Centre, Thailand, with the aim of equipping and releasing women to discover and fulfill their God-given role.

After attending a Transform Our World conference in Hawaii the previous year, and clearly hearing God's Word to me as a woman about stepping into my true identity, and helping other women around me to do the same, I came to understand how powerful it was to fully embrace our identity in Christ as His daughters. When we do this, it releases the potential we have to operate as God's Ekklesia, and effectively minister and bring the Kingdom of God near to others. As a women's group, we've been blessed with good sound biblical transformational resources. One such resource that has been a real blessing to us here in Phuket is Ruth Silvoso's book, Food, Family and Fun, *released in 2016.*

MARGARET BURTON

While it's a wonderful compilation of delicious and healthy recipes, it is also a collection of life-giving values designed to create a healthy and transformed lifestyle that will last. After reading and applying the principles in Ruth's book, I knew I could adapt it into a really good textbook to help teach women how to be intentional about seeing their family life transformed.

I developed a five-part series and took my Destiny group through it with the goal of inspiring the women to come to a place where their words and deeds were anointed by the Holy Spirit, and helping them to understand how to establish the Kingdom of God in every aspect of their personal lives: their marriages, their families and their spheres of influence.

The family is a very powerful expression of the Ekklesia. As wives, daughters and sisters who are envisioned and empowered, we become catalysts to bring change to our families. The Ekklesia begins in our homes and spreads to the marketplace. God has promised in His Word that where two or three are gathered in His Name, He is there (see Matthew 18:19,20). So, when you and your family gather around your kitchen table in His Name, God is there and your prayers are powerful. God will hear and answer because He loves you and your family.

In each session of my series, I covered one of these elements, together with a glimpse into Ruth's transformation lifestyle. I set a very clear goal for each session which included bringing out the main principles that Ruth is teaching. I also added a discussion time, prayer groups, and a challenge for the women to put into practice the following week what they had learned during the session. Each week we ate together, and had family and fellowship time with an appropriate activity to practically demonstrate what could be done in our respective family situations.

After introducing the main concepts of the book in Session One, I discovered that we had a lot of creativity in the group. Our ladies love calligraphy, and so it was fun to use these creative skills to write out Bible verses and also some of Ruth's quotes. During the activity the women talked with each other in an informal way, getting to know each other better, helping and encouraging each other, so that when it was time to gather in prayer groups it was very natural for them to share prayer needs and pray for each other. These activities allowed them to not only discover their creativity, but also gave them boldness to apply in their home what they had learned in the session, and to believe that they could see a change in their families.

In the group we had a wide variety of ages, nationalities, cultures, backgrounds and various expressions of the family, but everyone found the principles in Food, Family and Fun were applicable to their particular situation. As a result of this series we've seen the women grow and mature in the Lord, confident in their true identity in God, operating in the full anointing of the Holy Spirit. They have made prayer a part of their lifestyle, have been more intentional about finding ways to be together with their family that are fun and meaningful, and have also looked for ways to bless their neighbors and others in their sphere of influence.

MARGARET WITH HER DESTINY WOMEN'S GROUP

We've seen a husband come to church who didn't normally come. A grown-up daughter who hadn't been to church since she was a child heard about what we were doing and asked her mother if she could join us because she loved the craft she'd seen her mother doing in the home. Two new ladies have also joined the group. Two women who were on holiday in Phuket came to our morning service and changed their plans for the afternoon so that they could join us, and one lady came over from the mainland, driving 100km on her motorbike because she wanted to be part of it!

Can what we do really make a difference? Yes! As we make the decision to live in the anointing of the Holy Spirit and model godly principles in our home, we can have confidence that change will happen—starting with us, spreading to our home and our family—because a family that eats, has fun, prays and ministers together, not only stays together, but also has the potential to change the world!

I am amazed by how much God is using *Food, Family & Fun*, a book that I wrote originally to preserve memories of lessons we learned with Ed and our daughters around the dinner table. Like the young lad who gave his small lunch (five loaves and two fish) to Jesus and a hungry multitude was fed, God always multiplies what we put in His hands. Whatever is in your hands, place it in His today.

45 ARGENTINA: GOD'S GARDENER

My brother-in-law, Miguel Angel Pujol (Margarita's husband) is such a humble, easy-going man, but their influence in Corrientes, Argentina is extraordinary. He is very reluctant to talk much about what they do, but at my request he kindly wrote this faith-building account.

I received the title "Gardener of Souls" from the Director of Minority and Family Affairs of the Province of Corrientes, Argentina. It all started when I gathered my family to tell them of my decision to dedicate myself to gardening, for me an extraordinary job, a lovely journey in life.

Who would have imagined the reaction of one of my seven children (7-years-old at the time) who, with tears in his eyes, begged me not to do it. He said, "Daddy, in school they ask us what our fathers do and my classmates are the children of doctors, lawyers and entrepreneurs, and I don't want to say that my dad is a gardener."

After many years, today that son is the one who most enjoys what I do as a gardener. I design gardens and then I tell my employees how they should build them. This job takes me beyond what I could have imagined. Before becoming a Garden Designer, I had studied in Bible School and was a pastor in town. Gardening was going to be the way to support my wife and our seven children.

It all began when two journalists invited me to be on their radio program. Media was not my strong point but I decided to accept. The first words out of my mouth were: "I don't know how this will sound because I am closer to the ax and the machete than the microphone since I am a gardener." Then I proceeded to share how much I enjoy working as a gardener since it is a profession created by God.

Do you know who was listening at that very moment? The Governor of the Province of Corrientes! He did not delay a moment in instructing one of his deputies to invite me to take charge of the gardens at the Government Palace. Naturally, I accepted. Within a few days I was working at the highest level a gardener can aspire to. In addition to the residence of the Governor, I also oversaw gardens for the Vice Governor and other Ministers as well. None of that was a coincidence; God planned it that way.

Today I enjoy working those gardens as much as I did the first day. I built valuable friendships with government officials as a result of my work and my prayers for them. I always knew that the Lord had put me there.

We must be good stewards of everything God gives us and never overlook the opportunity to help others. Those good deeds please the Father. I learned at age 17 that life is eternal and that God has a purpose for us. That's a principle I still live by today.

I've been an Evangelical Pastor since I was very young and was always looking for an activity that would complement my Pastoral Ministry so I could be involved in the marketplace and not just inside the four walls of the church building. Now I work Monday through Friday on the gardens, and I dedicate the weekends to my family and to the church.

ED AND MIGUEL ANGEL

In 1993, on a Sunday morning, I left the regional hospital crying after spending time with the poor folks who slept on the staircases or in the corridors during the night because the hospitals in my city are not designed for the relatives of patients that come from far away in the interior of the province to accompany them when they are admitted.

That morning I promised the Lord that I would do everything possible to provide care and lodging for those who accompanied the patients or were receiving outpatient treatment but did not have the means to pay for lodging. I was reminded of what the Bible says in Acts 20:35: "By working hard in this manner you must help the weak and remember the words of the Lord Jesus…it is more blessed to give than to receive."

Considering what a gardener makes, this was a very big financial commitment, but I allowed myself to dream and I nurtured those dreams with prayer and dedication.

It took me seven long years to achieve the goal. In the Bible School where I studied public speaking and homiletics, the focus was the pulpit, but the Gospel message is best communicated through our lifestyle.

The audible dimension of the message is the preaching of the Gospel, but it's that invisible dimension—our lifestyle—that gives credibility to the audible. Jesus said something like this in John 10:37-38. Followers of Jesus have a two-part mission—first, to show Jesus. and second, to speak of Him.

The first home was inaugurated in the year 2000. We named it "My Brother's House" and it's a place where families of patients admitted to local hospitals can receive free food and lodging, and spiritual encouragement. Outpatients also have access to it during their recovery as if in their own home. Before that, if someone was receiving Chemotherapy as an outpatient, he or she would have to hang around and sit or sleep in the corridors of the hospital in between treatments.

"My Brother's House" is equipped with 57 beds, a large living room, kitchen, bathrooms, patios, dental and work-out equipment, hairdressers, and even an ambulance to transfer the deceased, along with their relatives, to their place of origin at no cost.

We also inaugurated "Casa de Padres," a facility that is similar to *La Casa de Mi Hermano* (the Spanish name for My Brother's House). This one is designed to support parents whose children are hospitalized in the Pediatric Hospital. This house is always full.

In 2010, "Hogar Esperanza" (Home of Hope, in English) was opened. It provides shelter and practical support and resources for those who are victims of domestic and gender violence.

All three Homes are open to the community 24/7 and they have room to care for up to 142 people at any one time.

These Homes have taught us innumerable lessons as we interact with people who, in the midst of suffering and dire economic limitations, do not give up but continue to "hang in there," hoping for a breakthrough. To comfort, listen and cry with them is an immense privilege and the words of Jesus are an inspiration: "To the extent that you did it to one of these brothers of mine, even the least of them, you did it to Me" (Matthew 25:40), and "Go and do the same" (Luke 10:37).

Love of neighbor is an essential command: God first, my neighbor second. We see this lived out in the story of the Good Samaritan who imitated our Lord Jesus when he went out of His way to love his neighbor and provided him with lodging and his basic needs.

The night we opened the doors of Hogar Esperanza and La Casa de Mi Hermano was very memorable because we were honored with the presence of the Governor and his wife, cabinet members, and business and community leaders in attendance.

It was exciting to share with them that the ministry of serving the poor and the needy is nothing more than following our Lord and obeying His commandments. I remember the moment the Governor approached me to inquire if we had a team of professionals to provide services in those Homes. When I informed him that we had a team of highly qualified Community Professionals who volunteer their services pro bono, as well as men and women from the church who share their testimonies of lives transformed by the love and power of God to infuse hope to the people who are staying with us, he was deeply impressed. I constantly thank God for the opportunity to serve Him by serving those in need, and the process to also influence the influencers.

MARGARITA AND MIGUEL ANGEL

ME AND MARGARITA

Another meaningful activity I organize each month is what we call "Breakfast for the Soul." These events allow me to cultivate friendships outside church circles and pray and minister to many who may never step foot inside a church.

The medical doctor who honored me with the title of "Gardener of Souls" wrote:

"The gardener managed to get many of us who were absorbed in our daily activities to turn our gaze to the brother who needs us as God did to the point of giving His Son for the good of all mankind. The gardener's commitment has become an expansive wave that now involves a significant number of people in our community."

My work of love is carried out with the support and companionship of the woman I married on April 20, 1963, in the City of Cordoba: Margarita Palau. She loves going to the House of My Brother where there are always those returning from the hospital with a heavy burden who need someone to talk to. She tells them about the Lord Jesus and prays with them, and they all get a taste of the Kingdom of God. They have been entrusted into our hands for a time and we should not miss the privilege and the opportunity to speak to them about God. This is what Jesus did when He was on earth, and it's what He commanded us to do as well.

Today Corrientes is a better place and scores of people have come to Christ because of the sacrificial obedience of this wonderful couple.

We had the privilege of donating an ambulance and a mobile medical clinic to their ministry. Those were some of the best investments we were able to facilitate because Miguel Angel and Margarita see Jesus every day in the "little ones" that Jesus described in Matthew chapter 25. Those are the down and out that society tends to overlook. But Miguel Angel and Margarita also minister to the upper class; their love and service has no limits. What an example of Christlikeness!

CORRIENTES SKYLINE

46 EGYPT: GOD MIGHTILY AT WORK

Egypt is a land that fascinates us because it is mentioned so often in the Bible. Also, because it's where Jesus and his parents were refugees after they fled Israel when an angel warned Joseph that Herod was planning to kill their baby.

We've had the opportunity to visit and minister in this country several times. Since Christians are a minority, they often have to endure tremendous pressure, and even persecution.

On one of those trips, we visited a church that operates in the largest garbage dump in the nation (El-Zabbaleen). When we first heard about its location we imagined an awful looking, miserable place. But when we went and met Father Samaan, we were blown away by how he and his congregation have transformed a dump into a clean and efficient processing center, creating jobs and even an expanding recycling industry.

We were so edified by the testimonies of conversions we heard. The Gospel is indeed the power of God to transform those that believe in Jesus, and also change their spheres of influence. What we saw demonstrates that such power is active in Egypt today.

On that same trip we had an equally satisfying experience at the other end of the social spectrum. A group of businesswomen in Cairo took us sailing on the Nile River and served us tea with delicious pastries on the deck of a beautiful boat. Admiring the banks of the river, I remembered the story of baby Moses and how he floated in a basket down that same river. It was a memorable time praying with these ladies for Egypt. They were so inspired that the next day they invited their friends, most of them influential ones, to a meeting in a private home where we shared the message of transformation.

All of that was very inspiring, but perhaps the story that touched our hears the most was the one about a young man who, after receiving Christ, was disowned by his parents and forced to move far away, severing all communication with him.

Some ten years later, the father became very ill and the family searched for a cure, to no avail. They had lost all hope when a neighbor told them about a preacher who prayed for the sick and many were healed, some from what doctors considered incurable diseases.

The parents figured that having tried everything within their possibilities, it wouldn't hurt to try one more time, even if it was a Christian preacher. When they went to the meetings, to their total astonishment they discovered that the healing evangelist was none other than the son they had disowned years earlier. The son prayed, and not only was the father healed, but the entire family came to faith in Christ.

God works in mysterious and marvelous ways indeed!

NILE RIVER

47 CALIFORNIA: WHEN PRIVATE EDUCATION GOES PUBLIC

Valley Christian Schools is an embassy of heaven in the San Francisco Bay Area. This is the school where our eldest daughter Karina serves the Lord as Executive Administrative Assistant to its President, Dr. Clifford Daugherty, a dear friend and co-worker in transformation. Also, Karina and Gary's children Vanessa, Sophia and Isabella graduated from the school. Vanessa is now a teacher there, and their youngest, Nathan, is an accomplished student and a Christian leader on campus.

CLIFFORD DAUGHERTY

Our other three daughters (Marilyn, Evelyn and Jesica) graduated from this school and were very active in the prayer and evangelism thrusts during their time there. Ed serves as chaplain to the Board of Directors and recently had the privilege, along with Dr. Daugherty, of commissioning the Board members as elders, the teachers as Ministers of Education, and the leadership team as ordained ministers. It was powerful!

For all practical purposes, Valley Christian Schools, under Dr. Daugherty's leadership, has become an Ekklesia, as you will see in the next story from Ed's book *Ekklesia: Rediscovering God's Instrument for Global Transformation.*

In the early 1990s, Dr. Clifford Daugherty and his school board were struggling to keep Valley Christian Schools in San Jose, California, afloat, subsisting on rented public school campus facilities and carrying a deficit in the hundreds of thousands of dollars. But exposure to the principles of transformation that had changed Resistencia, Argentina, baptized him with hope and put him in touch with a new authority. Upon returning home from a Transform Our World global conference, he decided to move on what he had learned, first by gathering with intercessors, and then by engaging the student body in prayer evangelism to change the spiritual climate on campus.

Shortly after that initial point of inception was established, the powers of darkness began to recede. The financial deficit was taken care of. The suppressed hope for a new campus took on new life. Today, Valley Christian Schools is housed on a $200 million campus and is considered by some to be the top-rated school in the nation. Its accelerated programs in science and math are allowing *students to launch their own experiments to the International Space Station. It was then that Dr. Daugherty experienced a new illumination: To whom much is given, much will be required. What can we do for public education?*

Inspiration came to establish a Junior University and Lighthouse Initiative that involves sending Valley Christian student mentors every week to a local public school to assist underprivileged students with skill development, tutoring and extracurricular activities.

The results were outstanding. Hellyer Elementary School Principal Jerry Merza reported that in the fifth year of the program, "we catapulted ourselves to above [the state-mandated score of] 800, which was a huge accomplishment." Hellyer went from being one of the lowest-performing schools in the county to being among the top five in two counties in their socioeconomic bracket.[8]

That the mentoring program provided influence at the relational and motivational levels was tremendous, but what about at the spiritual level? Dr. Daugherty confessed, "It was my opinion, like many Christians, that there wasn't much hope for our public schools because we didn't feel that [because of Church and State regulations] we could have much of an influence."

That mindset derived from the U.S. Supreme Court rulings of 1962–63 to prohibit prayer in the schools, and by default, anything that had to do with religion. Dr. Daugherty recounts, "When I lodged my complaint [to the Lord], I sensed an immediate reply: So you think the highest law in the land is the United States Supreme Court?"

Dr. Daugherty admitted his faithlessness and immediately felt the Holy Spirit speaking to him again: Why don't you put the rulings of 1962 and 1963 on appeal to the Supreme Court Judge of the Heavens and Earth? I'll take the case.[9]

The heavens opened as Dr. Daugherty shifted from a natural power perspective to a supernatural authority mindset. God began to peel away in his mind the many misconceptions about how those rulings could impede what God wanted to do in public education, and He poured in new concepts and ideas. Among these was a music program based on the words of the Declaration of Independence that would develop a common virtues-oriented relationship with the public schools: "We hold these truths to be self-evident, that all men are created equal, that they are endowed by their Creator with certain unalienable Rights, that among these are Life, Liberty and the Pursuit of Happiness."

Those words suddenly sounded very similar to "righteousness, peace and joy" to Dr. Daugherty—the very components of the Kingdom of God. Valley Christian Schools was off and running, and the doors of influence and favor continued to increase.

Today, the school is a functional Ekklesia, even though the word is not used. It exerts a rapidly growing outward ripple of authority that is ministering to the felt needs of multiple public

It is amazing what God can do when we say yes...

---

[8] Dr. Clifford Daugherty, *The Quest Continues: Light, Life and Learning* (Quest for Excellence Media, 2015), 64.

[9] Ibid

schools, even to the point of sharing the resources of its Applied Math Science and Engineering Institute to help other schools put science projects in space, something they otherwise would not be able to do. The initial breakthrough at Hellyer Elementary led the superintendent and the Franklin McKinley School District to become a member of the Quest Institute for Quality Education, opening the door for even more goodness, peace and joy. As a result, the new mentoring programs have led to the establishment of Kids Clubs on those campuses.

It is amazing what God can do when we say yes to His command to disciple not only people, but also institutions. Since this private school "went public" by investing time and resources in the nearby public schools, over four thousand decisions for Christ have been reported.

More amazing yet, so far, all of the baptisms of students from local public high schools have taken place in the pool at Andrew Hill High School. That is possible because the Court of Heaven overruled the earthly court. Awesome!

VALLEY CHRISTIAN SCHOOLS CAMPUS, SAN JOSE, CALIFORNIA

48 HONG KONG: EKKLESIA FOR MILLENNIALS

A young millennial couple in Hong Kong decided to apply the principles of Ekklesia in the most creative way using the business they started as the launching pad. AMENPAPA is an unabashedly Christian fashion brand that is making waves in Hong Kong and throughout the Asian fashion world. This business uses clothes and accessories as the canvas to display the Word of God and they are the "hippest thing happening" according to what you read about them on the Internet!

Geoff Poon, and his wife Salina, founded AMENPAPA to demonstrate how the Kingdom of God extends far beyond the four walls of the conventional church. Planted in the marketplace, following the leading of the Holy Spirit, and thinking outside the box, they are transforming lives and influencing their industry niche.

The initial concept came as a result of how Salina met Jesus. She had been struggling with depression and no matter how hard she tried she couldn't shake it. Living from one day to the next was a challenge. What God used to get through to her was a billboard that displayed Bible verses and encouraging messages. She would look for those each day, and that kept her going. Eventually, she heard the Gospel and she and Geoff gave not only their hearts, but also their business to the Lord, and as a result many have been impacted.

When Ed and I were visiting one of their stores in Hong Kong, we heard about a famous singer who went there one day, very interested because he saw words from the Bible imprinted on the clothes and other articles in a very contemporary and eye-catching way. He asked if the owners were Christians and that opened the door for one of the workers to minister to him. As a result, he came back to the Lord after many years away from Him.

We continue to hear inspiring stories about this couple who minister in the marketplace, bringing God's Kingdom to the fashion industry in such a creative way.

49 CHRISTIAN FOOTPRINTS ON THE MOON

In 1972, we had the privilege of spending time with Colonel James Irwin, one of the twelve men from the Apollo program that walked on the moon. Over dinner one evening he shared about this experience.

James told us what a special feeling it was to contemplate his footprints on the moon and to look down and see the earth the size of a marble. He was enthralled by its beauty, and although it was so far away, he felt strangely at home on the moon.

During Apollo 15, the lunar mission he was a part of with two other astronauts, Christians in his church, and many around the world, were praying for him and his partners. He could feel the power of God and he knew that He was there with them. He told us how God guided them to find the now famous "Genesis Rock," which is on display at the Lunar Sample Laboratory Facility in Houston, Texas[10]. The white rock was sitting on top of another rock, beaming in the sun, as if to shout, "Here I am. Pick me up!"

GENESIS ROCK

Irwin had graduated from test pilot school in 1961 and considered himself the "coolest" pilot in the sky, but one day he crashed his plane and there went his ego. He and the others on board were seriously injured (broken legs, broken jaw, teeth knocked out, multiple concussions and lacerations). The doctors told him that he probably wouldn't fly again.

In his despair, James cried out to God, and during his lengthy hospital stay, he prayed for healing and understanding. Having received Christ as his Savior when he was very young, he knew that Jesus loved him. In time, God healed him and helped him to fly again.

[10] https://en.wikipedia.org/wiki/Genesis_Rock

James loved speed and taking risks, so he enrolled in the space program. After training and preparing for five years, he was ready to go to the moon. He said, "My flight through life has been sustained by the power of my knowledge of Jesus."

He also told us, "When I was on the moon, I was inspired to quote from Psalm 121: 'My help comes from the Lord, who made heaven and earth.' He made the moon and made it possible for me to place my footprints there.

As fascinating as that experience was, I believe that Jesus Christ walking on the earth 2000 years ago, and now dwelling in our midst through the Holy Spirit, is far more important than any man walking on the moon."

Those are impressive words, coming from someone who was privileged to leave his footprints on the moon. Jesus wants to walk in your life today. All you have to do is call upon Him to have life and have it abundantly (John 10:10), and when you die you will be transported beyond the moon into God's presence in heaven.

50 CHARLES DUKE OF THE APOLLO 16 MISSION

Ed and I went to a Prayer Breakfast where we heard the inspiring testimony of Charles Duke, another one of the few men who left footprints on the moon. He was the lunar module pilot for the Apollo 16 mission. He said, "After walking on the moon, I had fame, fortune and a spot in the history books. I had it all. Still, I was failing miserably as a husband and father. I knew Jesus the way you know the U.S. presidents—by name only."

After the Apollo mission, he retired and started a business that succeeded with money rolling in, but he was bored. He noticed that his wife had changed; she had joy and no longer suffered from depression. She had turned to God for answers to her problems. One day, Duke went with her to a home group meeting where they were discussing the topic of *Who is Jesus?* He could only answer that He was the Son of God, but he had never trusted in Him.

That day, as the group dove into the Scriptures and various members shared their personal testimonies, he came face to face with the opportunity to follow Jesus. When they returned home, he prayed with his wife and gave his life over to Him. Right then and there he knew that Jesus was real, and the next day he woke up with a great desire to read the Bible.

Duke once said, "It cost the government $400 million for me to walk three days on the moon, and then it was over. But to walk with Jesus is free and it lasts forever!"

51 HAWAII: THE WITCH THAT QUIT

Joy Chinen is a dear personal friend of mine. She and her husband Cal are also very dear to our family. They practice prayer evangelism and the transformation principles at home and in the church they lead. Cal already shared in a separate story how the insights into the Ekklesia helped him become a more effective pastor which empowered the members of his congregation to take the power and the presence of God to their spheres of influence.

The following testimony from Joy demonstrates how the Gates of Hades cannot prevail against the Ekklesia.

One of the women in our Ekklesia group works as an usher in one of the conference centers in town and a well-known psychic was coming to put on a show there. My friend was glad that she was off that night, but at the last minute she got called in to cover for a co-worker. She really didn't want to do it, but they begged her to come in.

While she was ushering, she quietly declared God's peace and blessings over the meeting room. This is something she learned to do when she realized she was a minister in her workplace. During the show, the medium "saw" (as was customary during her shows) "something" in a certain part of the room and said there was a spirit of suicide. The woman sitting right in front of the medium was crying. It was obvious that she was struggling with suicidal thoughts.

Suddenly, the medium spoke out in frustration, declaring she could not continue, and abruptly ending the show. My friend heard the Holy Spirit tell her to go and pray for the woman that was crying. She went to where the woman was standing with four others, and asked if she could pray for her. Without hesitation, the woman agreed. Hearing this, one of the other women said, "Yes, let's pray."

When they got into a circle, there was silence and she was waiting for someone to pray out loud, but no one did. When she looked up, the other ladies told her that she should pray. She did, and the distraught woman immediately felt better. After everyone left the room, those ladies found my friend again since she was ushering people out of the building.

"We didn't know that you worked here!" they exclaimed. "We've never had an employee, let alone an usher, pray for people attending events. Thank you!"

Whatever spiritual challenges are thrown at you, remember that "Greater is He who is in you than he who is in the world" (1 John 4:4). Jesus is building the Church, His Ekklesia, and He was emphatic that the Gates of Hades would not prevail against us, and they don't when we go there as His Ekklesia!

CAL & JOY CHINEN ARE SUCH A BLESSING

52 LOS ANGELES: THE GANG THAT RETURNED THE STOLEN KEYBOARD

In 2019, we were ministering at a church in the Los Angeles area and the pastor told us this story:

> When I was young, I used to visit juvenile jails to minister to and pray for young people in trouble. Many of them received the Lord.
>
> After I got married, my wife and I started this church, and soon after, somebody broke in and stole our keyboard. I went to the corner where there was a group of punk kids and told them, "Somebody stole the keyboard from our church. I know you must know about it. Who did it?"
>
> They looked at me with murderous intentions…one of them pulled out a knife and sneered, "We didn't steal your piano, pastor, so get lost…or else!"
>
> I realized the danger I was in but felt that I needed to hold my ground. A stand-off ensued until one of the guys in the gang said, "Hold on, don't do anything to him. I know this man. He is good. He used to visit me in jail. Don't hurt him; let him go."
>
> It wasn't long before the keyboard was back at the church, and a backsliding believer got a call to come home.

The Bible says, "Cast your bread on the surface of the waters, for you will find it after many days" (Ecclesiastes 11:1). When you help others, you are bound to be blessed in return, even if it takes some time.

53 THE CASE OF TWO STOLEN BICYCLES PLUS ONE GUITAR

Dave and Sue Thompson are dear friends. They have worked with us from the very beginning of our ministry, when we were building the retreat center in Argentina. Later on, they moved to Resistencia where Dave was the onsite director for Plan Resistencia, the prayer evangelism thrust that produced tremendous church growth as I shared before.

The story Dave tells below shows again how small beginnings, when placed in God's hands, produce great outcomes.

Shortly after we moved to Resistencia, a wayward teen scaled a 6-foot wall and stole Tim and Christi's bicycles. We were staying in a guest apartment at Pastor Alejandro's church. The kids cried uncontrollably when they found out their beautiful bikes were gone. Not having any other recourse, I prayed a Carlos Annacondia-type prayer with them, rebuking the devil, calling down the power of heaven, declaring the bikes to be instruments of transformation and blessing the thief, claiming him for the kingdom. I had never prayed like that before!

DAVE AND SUE THOMPSON

TIM THOMPSON AND HIS BIKE

But nothing happened. The bikes never came back nor were they ever found. And no bike thief came into the kingdom.

However, ten years later, long after we had returned to live in the U.S., a young man stood with his wife and two daughters to give testimony in Pastor Alejandro's church about how they had come to the Lord through a home group from the church that came out of the "Houses of Light" prayer movement we had initiated during Plan Resistencia. At the end of his testimony, he turned to the pastor and said, "I also want to apologize to you, Pastor, because ten years ago, I climbed over the wall behind the church and stole two of your bicycles. I have asked God to forgive me, and now I ask you."

Pastor Alejandro immediately sent us word that our prayers had been completely answered, with interest paid. Not only did the thief come into the kingdom, but he brought an entire family with him!

Years later, Christi's son, Federico, was studying at Bible School in Redding, California. Being a musician, he had left a very expensive bass guitar and pedals he had borrowed from a friend in the trunk of his car while he went into a meeting. When he came out, the trunk was ajar and the equipment was missing. He was shaken because the hundreds of dollars it would cost to replace the guitar was a fortune to him. He called home to Argentina to talk to his mom. She reminded him of the story about the stolen bicycles. They prayed the same prayer over the stolen guitar.

The next day, Federico got a call from the owner of a music store that he frequented in the city. They had become good friends and Federico had told him of the incident. The owner texted him a picture of a guitar that someone had just brought into the store in hopes of reselling it. The storeowner became suspicious and remembered Federico. The equipment was miraculously recovered. Law enforcement officials immediately showed up to "disciple" the thieves according to the law, and all of us learned the power of generational blessings. "We are a chosen lineage...to announce the virtues of Him who called us out of darkness to his marvelous light" (1 Peter 2:9).

It is amazing and encouraging to see how God uses past miracles to inspire us—in this case Dave and Sue's daughter and their grandson—to believe for a miracle today. The Gospel is indeed the power of God!

THE THOMPSON FAMILY

54 THE ICE CREAM LADY AND THE PROVINCIAL MAYOR

Ed always says, "There may be people better qualified than us to do the work of the Lord, but when He chooses us, we become the best ones for the job, not because of our skills, but because *He chose us.*"

This story is unique yet beautiful and powerful.

In Phuket, Thailand, a woman named Wanlapa was a medium—sort of a witch doctor— dying of cancer who, in desperation, called on a British missionary that had been serving faithfully in this Buddhist nation. The pastor she called on is the one who rebuilt the Muslim school. This is the story of how they met and how God used them to impact the highest sphere of government in their province.

When they first met, Wanlapa asked Pastor Brian Burton if he would take care of her youngest daughter, Gip, after she passed away. Brian assured her that he would, but he also told her, "I am going to pray and God will heal you." She believed and was healed instantly.

Obviously, she couldn't go back to her old job as a medium, so Pastor Brian bought her an ice cream cart and encouraged her to make a living by selling ice cream. Wanlapa testified often to her customers about her miraculous healing but did not succeed in leading anyone to the Lord. Such was the spiritual darkness oppressing the region!

One day, Brian heard a friend talking about our ministry and she gave him Ed's book *Anointed for Business*. After he'd read it, his friend tried for two years to convince him to attend our Global Conference in Argentina (where they were held until 2008). Finally, in 2007 she paid for him to go herself. During the conference he realized that he was sent by God to Thailand not just to plant a church, but also to reach his city and the nation. He read Ed's other book *Transformation* and went back to teach his congregation the principles found in both books.

The "Ice Cream Lady" (Wanlapa) heard the message and realized, *I am anointed for business; my ice creams are like arrows in the hands of a mighty warrior and this is not an ice cream cart but a chariot of fire. I can change the spiritual climate everywhere I go with my cart and pray for every person that buys ice cream from me.* Armed with this new understanding, she became instrumental in leading many people to the Lord and encouraged others to do the same.

Seven hundred people came to Christ in the first year alone, and many thousands after that. This growth was extraordinary when compared to the 43 members that the previous 16 years of missionary work by the Burtons had produced, but her pastor now understood that the ultimate objective was not to build a mega-church, but to transform the nation. And this is what he began to teach his growing congregation.

With this in mind, Wanlapa, a faithful disciple, parked her ice cream cart outside the Provincial Mayor's offices and prayed for him regularly. She knew that even if he didn't know it, she knew that she was his pastor, and she blessed him every time she was selling outside his office.

One day, she saw the Provincial Mayor and told him, "I have been blessing you. You should come to my church." He must have felt the anointing emanating from her because he agreed and asked for the church address!

THE FAMOUS ICE CREAM CART

The next Sunday, Pastor Brian was speaking on one of the paradigms he heard Ed teach about at the conference he'd attended: to eliminate poverty it is necessary to uproot corruption. He looked out at the congregation and there was the Provincial Mayor, the one considered by many as the most corrupt person in Phuket.

Brian whispered a prayer under his breath, "Lord, can I change the message? He can revoke my visa and then we'll be forced to leave this country that you brought us to."

He heard the Lord reply, "Well, I can revoke your next breath…" So, he preached on how to uproot corruption!

The Provincial Mayor kept his head down during the sermon and left as soon as it was over. Brian told Margaret, "Honey, you better pack because he's going to kick us out of the country."

**WANLAPA, AKA
"THE ICE CREAM LADY"**

On Wednesday, Pastor Brian got a call from the Provincial Mayor inviting him to lunch. Brian said, "Great, he's inviting me to lunch before he kicks us out of here."

But his concern was unfounded. At lunch, the Provincial Mayor, very convicted, told Brian, "I was at your church on Sunday…"

"Yes, I noticed," Brian replied.

"And I didn't like what you said because this month I took a million-dollar bribe to authorize the construction of a hospital. As I listened to your sermon, I realized that I didn't take the bribe from the hospital, but from the poor people in Phuket who will receive inferior services." Under tremendous conviction for his misdeed, he asked Pastor Brian, "Do you think Jesus can forgive me?"

> She knew that even if he wasn't aware of it, she was his pastor, and she blessed him every time she was selling outside his office.

Brian led him to the Lord, and at that moment the Provincial Mayor reached under the table and pulled out a bag containing a million dollars. Subsequently, another half million was returned by the manager of the construction company, and eventually over seven million dollars in bribes were returned and used to help the poor.

The Ice Cream Lady continued taking the message of Jesus to village after village until she heard about ministering in jails. She went to the maximum-security prison and told the guards that she had a message that would help the prisoners. At first, they told her to get lost, but she persisted and wouldn't take no for an answer. Eventually she got in, and through her ministry the spiritual climate changed completely and miracles happened regularly.

All this took place because a humble woman decided to obey God. He can use anyone who is willing to be used! Are you? I hope so!

THE PROVINCIAL MAYOR ENJOYED ED'S BOOK!

From my heart

I pray that this selection of pages from our own journey has blessed and encouraged you on yours. I have shared candidly and sincerely, not shying away from the difficult and sometimes unpleasant experiences. Life this side of heaven is a challenge, but we never walk alone. The Lord is our strength, and even if He may occasionally be silent, He is never absent. He holds our hand, and when we fall, He picks us up and holds us close to His heart.

As this book comes to an end, I fervently pray that first and foremost you invite the Lord to come into your heart if you haven't done it already because, "As many as received Him, to them He gave the right to become children of God" (John 1:12). This is the most important decision a human being can ever make. It is what sustained my mother and my siblings when I was growing up, and it is what continues to sustain me and my family when the winds turn fierce and the waves threaten to drown us.

It was a simple and short prayer that saved Peter when he began to sink: "Lord, save me!" (Matthew 14:30b). Short and straight to the point, and as a result of that cry for help, Jesus grabbed his hand, lifted him up and walked with him back to the boat as the sea calmed. That's the kind of life He has in store for you. To access it, pray this prayer: "Lord Jesus, I need you. On the Cross you shed your blood to pay the price for my sins. Please come into my heart and live in it forever as my Lord and Savior." Do it now and it will change your life forever.

I close by quoting the words that God chose to bless His people when they were walking in the wilderness on their way to the Promised Land, not unlike the journey that you and I are embarked on today:

The Lord bless you and keep you;
The Lord make His face shine on you,
And be gracious to you;
The Lord lift up His countenance on you
And give you peace.

Numbers 6:24-26

Ruth

ACKNOWLEDGEMENTS

I want to thank the Lord from the bottom of my heart for allowing me to pen this book. I felt His presence and guidance all along. To Him I give all the honor and glory.

I also wish to thank Ed, the love of my life. He is as handsome and spiritual today as he was when I first met him, and even more so because time has added maturity and wisdom to his wonderful character.

His prayers, encouragement and advice helped me stay focused. Thank you, darling. You are the best!

My profound gratitude to our daughters, sons-in-law and grandchildren for the joy they bring to my life and their inspiring examples that are reflected in these pages. Thank you also to our friends in the Kingdom of God who contributed stories, and a special thank you to our partners in Transform Our World, Cindy Oliveira and Dave Thompson, and Andrew Isaacs of i6Graphics, who assisted me immensely in readying the manuscript for publication.

WHAT LEADERS ARE SAYING ABOUT
FOOD, FAMILY & FUN

"Imagine my amazement, at 30,000 feet on the way back to Cincinnati, when I opened your book. First of all, Ruth, it is exceptional in every way. I loved learning more about your family history, and the traditions you and Ed have built into your household. But more than that, the entire format—down to every detail—was perfectly rendered. I literally had all the flight attendants gathered around my seat as I read through the pages! They were as fascinated as I was, and when we got to the photo of the dish with the carrots, one of the attendants quipped that while she didn't even like carrots, the photo was enough for her to give them another try. I sent every one of them to the TOW website to buy the book!"

– Chuck Proudfit

"Sooooo so wonderful...I'm feeling joyful and emotional just reading all the precious ways Ruth has brightened the role of wife and mother and loving chef! She's truly been my most multifaceted example. We love you and rejoice over the book and bless it as it goes out into homes. I especially loved Ed's de-votion page to Ruth!"

– Danielle Guzman

"I just wanted to let you know that I started talking and preaching out of Ruth's book two Sundays ago and started taking orders for Ruth's book. Yesterday, I read from the section entitled "The family that prays together stays together," and we received 57 orders! We are so blessed. Thank you so much for doing this book. It is the perfect companion to Ed's Ekklesia *book."*

– Pastor Cal Chinen

"*Food, Family and Fun is an absolute winner! I LOVE it! The balance of good food, uplifting stories, prayer, and family fellowship is wonderful. Many congratulations, Ruth, and to the whole family.*"

– Dr. Caroline Oda

"*I just love the Food, Family and Fun book. I share the same passion for food and family with Mother Ruth. There are many recipes that I can adapt for my office lunch! It is such a wonderful book and will be loved by many. Other than the recipes, the stories are just as good, and the pictures, too. So well done. I am floored by the perfect layout and the content. Mother Ruth, you are my hero!!*"

– Mimi Chan

"*I received the four copies of your new book yesterday, Ruth, and it is absolutely beautiful. What a treasure! I will give one to Colleen, daughter Sarah, and daughters-in-law, Leah and Sarah for Christmas, and plan to share the concept of planting an Ekklesia in our homes with them all on Christmas Day, along with some special prayer time with the whole family. Thank you so much for the love of Jesus that comes through this beautiful book so loud and clear. I, too, look forward to reading every page (and trying every recipe).*"

– Pastor Greg Pagh

"*Life should be a beautiful piece of art, and this book represents that reality like no other. Thank you, Ruth, for the love you put into the pages of Food, Family and Fun.*"

– Beni Johnson

"*Ruth Silvoso has tapped into secrets that, when applied, will bring delight not only to your table, but to the whole family! The stories of cooking, mixed with a strong dose of love and family, are needed ingredients in every kitchen and house.*"

– Cindy Jacobs

CONTACT THE AUTHOR

Ruth Palau Silvoso | TRANSFORM OUR WORLD
P.O. Box 20310 San Jose, CA 95160–0310

Email: ruthsilvoso@transformourworld.org

Visit our website for inspiring resources and events:
www.transformourworld.org